Company's Coming ®

SALADS

by
Jean Paré

Cover Photo

1. Japanese Chicken Salad page 132
2. Lemon Cheddar Salad page 87
3. Spinach Salad page 11

SALADS

Fifteenth Edition January, 1991

I.S.B.N. 0-9690695-3-7

Published and Distributed by
Company's Coming Publishing Limited
Box 8037, Station "F"
Edmonton, Alberta, Canada
T6H 4N9

Printed in Canada

Cookbooks in the Company's Coming series by Jean Paré:

English Hard Cover Title

 JEAN PARÉ'S FAVORITES
VOLUME ONE

English Soft Cover Titles

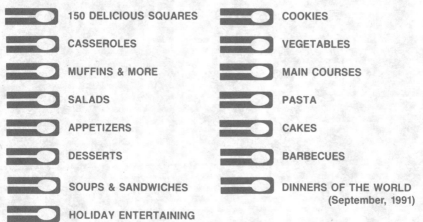

150 DELICIOUS SQUARES   COOKIES

CASSEROLES   VEGETABLES

MUFFINS & MORE   MAIN COURSES

SALADS   PASTA

APPETIZERS   CAKES

DESSERTS   BARBECUES

SOUPS & SANDWICHES   DINNERS OF THE WORLD
(September, 1991)

HOLIDAY ENTERTAINING

Cookbooks in the Jean Paré series:

French Soft Cover Titles

150 DÉLICEUX CARRÉS

LES CASSEROLES

MUFFINS ET PLUS

table of Contents

Jean Paré was born and raised during the Great Depression in Irma, a small farm town in eastern Alberta. She grew up understanding that the combination of family, friends and home cooking is the essence of a good life. Jean learned from her mother, Ruby Elford, to appreciate good cooking and was encouraged by her father, Edward Elford, who praised even her earliest attempts. When she left home she took with her many acquired family recipes, her love of cooking and her intriguing desire to read recipe books like novels!

While raising a family of four, Jean was always busy in her kitchen preparing delicious, tasty treats and savory meals for family and friends of all ages. Her reputation flourished as the mom who could happily feed the neighborhood.

In 1963, when her children had all reached school age, Jean volunteered to cater to the 50th anniversary of the Vermilion School of Agriculture, now Lakeland College. Working out of her home, Jean prepared a dinner for over 1000 people which launched a flourishing catering operation that continued for over eighteen years. During that time she was provided with countless opportunities to test new ideas with immediate feedback – resulting in empty plates and contented customers! Whether preparing cocktail sandwiches for a house party or serving a hot meal for 1500 people, Jean Paré earned a reputation for good food, courteous service and reasonable prices.

"Why don't you write a cookbook?" Time and again Jean was asked that question as requests for her recipes mounted. Jean's response was to team up with her son Grant Lovig in the fall of 1980 to form Company's Coming Publishing Limited. April 14, 1981 marked the debut of "150 DELICIOUS SQUARES", the first Company's Coming cookbook in what soon would become Canada's most popular cookbook series. Jean released a new title each year for the first six years. The pace quickened and by 1987 the company had begun publishing two titles each year.

Jean Paré's operation has grown from the early days of working out of a spare bedroom in her home to operating a large and fully equipped test kitchen in Vermilion, near the home she and her husband Larry built. Full time staff has grown steadily to include marketing personnel located in major cities across Canada. Home office is located in Edmonton, Alberta where distribution, accounting and administration functions are headquartered. Company's Coming cookbooks are now distributed throughout Canada and the United States plus numerous overseas markets.

Jean Paré's approach to cooking has always called for easy-to-follow recipes using mostly common, affordable ingredients. Her wonderful collection of time-honored recipes, many of which are family heirlooms, is a welcome addition to any kitchen. That's why we say: taste the tradition.

*To those who recognize the value of nutrition
but haven't forgotten that food should be tasty and fun.*

Foreword

With the great variety of salads these days, we can easily find one to suit the alloted time for preparation. They fit into any menu and are available year round.

No other type of food preparation lends itself so readily to creativity. Virtually any food can be added to a salad of one kind or another.

Molded salads call for imagination. Try making them in all sorts of molds, bowls, glasses, etc. They are very showy and add greatly to the appearance of any table. Being able to make them ahead is a distinct advantage to busy cooks. A full metric measure is not always used in the jellied salads so as to ensure that the correct proportions of liquid and gelatin are maintained. Flavored gelatin used in the recipes is also known as Jello jelly powder.

A well stocked shelf is convenient and allows imagination to go to work with canned fruit, vegetables, seafood, meat and fruit juices.

Fresh greens appeal to everyone. Using at least two types of lettuce gives more interest. Crisp green salads add to any menu. Several Caesar Salad recipes are included for your perusal. This combines flair with economy.

Be aware of the difference between mayonnaise and salad dressing, mayonnaise being the milder of the two.

Salads, with the exception of those which are served in the frozen state, should be served fresh.

Check your salad fixings. Company's coming!

Jean Paré

This has a thick creamy dressing. Excellent salad.

DRESSING

Garlic clove	1	1
Large egg (or 2 smaller)	1	1
Worcestershire sauce	1 tsp.	5 mL
Lemon juice	2 tbsp.	30 mL
Anchovie paste	2 tsp.	10 mL
Dash of pepper		
Cooking oil	1 cup	250 mL

Put first six ingredients into blender. Blend until smooth. With blender running add cooking oil in a slow stream. Chill about 2 hours.

SALAD

Large head romaine lettuce	1	1
Croutons	2 cups	500 mL
Bacon slices, cooked and crumbled	8	8
Parmesan cheese	½ cup	125 mL

Tear lettuce in bite size pieces in salad bowl. Add croutons. Add dressing. Toss to coat.

Sprinkle with bacon and cheese.

CROUTONS

Butter or margarine	2 tbsp.	30 mL
Garlic clove, sliced	1	1
White bread slices, cubed	4-5	4-5

Saute garlic in butter for 2-3 minutes. Remove garlic and discard. Add bread cubes. Fry until golden, stirring often. Remove. Cool.

Pare Pointer

Politeness is a great air cushion — even empty it eases the jolt.

SPINACH MAKE AHEAD

This is a green salad that can be made "the day before".

Large bunch spinach leaves	1	1
Swiss cheese, shredded or cubed	½ cup	125 mL
Cheddar cheese, shredded or cubed	½ cup	125 mL
Mushrooms, sliced	2 cups	500 mL
Hard boiled eggs, sliced	4	4
Mayonnaise	1 cup	250 mL
Sour cream	½ cup	125 mL
Milk	3 tbsp.	50 mL
Lemon juice	2 tsp.	10 mL
Granulated sugar	2 tsp.	10 mL
Green onions, sliced thin	¼ cup	50 mL
Bacon slices, cooked and crumbled	4	4

Arrange torn up clean spinach leaves in bottom of medium size glass bowl. Put cheese cubes on top. Spread mushrooms over cheese. Cover with sliced eggs.

In small bowl cream together well, mayonnaise, sour cream, milk, lemon juice and sugar. Stir in onions. Spread over top of salad right to the sides of bowl. Cover. Chill overnight. To serve, remove cover, sprinkle bacon over top.

ROMAINE MAKE AHEAD: Omit spinach and use Romaine lettuce in above salad. Every bit as good.

Variation: Omit mayonnaise and sour cream. Add 8 oz. (250 g) cream cheese mixed with ½ cup (125 mL) sour cream.

LETTUCE TOMATO

A pretty salad to brighten appetites.

Lettuce, solid medium head	¼	¼
Green onions, chopped	2-3	2-3
Tomatoes cut in small chunks	1-2	1-2
Salad dressing to coat		

Cut or tear lettuce in small pieces in salad bowl. Add green onions. Add tomatoes just before serving so as not to dilute dressing. Add salad dressing. Toss to coat. Serves 4.

Not the usual spinach salad. Different and tastier.

DRESSING

Commercial salad dressing	½ cup	125 mL
Commercial coleslaw dressing	¼ cup	50 mL
Dried dill weed	¼ tsp.	1 mL

Combine all together. Stir. Set aside.

SALAD

Large bunch of spinach leaves	1	1
Swiss cheese, shredded	¼ cup	50 mL
Cheddar cheese, shredded	¼ cup	50 mL
Sliced mushrooms	1 cup	250 mL
Bacon slices, cooked and crumbled	6	6
Hard boiled eggs, chopped	2	2

Tear clean spinach leaves into large bowl. Add about three quarters dressing. Toss to coat. Pile on four to six salad plates.

Sprinkle shredded cheese over top followed by mushrooms, crumbled bacon and chopped egg. Drizzle a bit of dressing over top. Serve immediatley. Serves 4-6.

Pictured on cover.

Variation: Omit Swiss and increase Cheddar to ½ cup (125 mL), shredded for equally good results.

ROMAINE SALAD: Substitute Romaine lettuce for the spinach leaves. Delicious and easier to obtain at times than spinach.

Pare Pointer

Vampires only play baseball at night 'cause that's when the bats come out.

WILTED LETTUCE

A terrific way to use leaf lettuce although head lettuce can also be used.

Lettuce (tear up leaf lettuce, shred head lettuce)	6 cups	1.5 L
Bacon slices, diced	4	4
Green onions, sliced	4	4
Salt	½ tsp.	2 mL
Pinch pepper		
Vinegar	3 tbsp.	50 mL
Water	3 tbsp.	50 mL
Brown sugar	2 tbsp.	30 mL
Hard boiled egg (optional garnish)	1	1

Put lettuce in salad bowl.

Fry bacon until crisp stirring occasionally. Add onions, salt, pepper, vinegar, water and sugar. Stir. Bring to boil. Pour over lettuce. Toss until coated and wilted. Scatter egg over top. Serve immediately.

WILTED SPINACH: Omit lettuce and add large bunch of spinach.

WILTED ROMAINE: Substitute a large head of Romaine lettuce for the leaf or head lettuce.

EASIER CAESAR

When time is at a premium and salad makings are not complete, you will find this a great short-cut.

Large head of Romaine lettuce or your choice of greens	8 cups	2 L
Croutons	2 cups	500 mL
Commercial Caesar dressing	½ cup	125 mL

Tear greens in bite size pieces in salad bowl. Add croutons. Add dressing. Adjust amount according to amount of greens used. Toss and serve. Serves 4-6.

Great for those wishing to have just a bit of garlic.

Garlic clove, halved	1	1
Large head Romaine lettuce	1	1
Croutons (see below)	2 cups	500 mL
Grated Parmesan cheese	½ cup	125 mL

DRESSING

Cider vinegar	¼ cup	50 mL
Egg yolk	1	1
Cooking oil	⅓ cup	75 mL
Anchovies, chopped (optional)	4-6	4-6
Grated Parmesan cheese	¼ cup	50 mL
Prepared mustard	1 tsp.	5 mL

Rub inside of salad bowl with garlic — as little or as much as you like. Remove garlic. Tear lettuce into bite size pieces into salad bowl. Add croutons and first amount of cheese.

Combine vinegar, egg yoke, oil, anchovies, second amount of cheese and mustard in small bowl. Mix well. Pour over salad. Toss and serve. Serves 6.

Note: Shrimp may be substituted in place of anchovies. Use fresh or tinned. Amount will vary depending on how many people you are serving.

CROUTONS

Garlic clove, halved (or ½ tsp., 2 mL, garlic salt)	1	1
Cooking oil	2 tbsp.	30 mL
Cubed bread (French bread is best)	2 cups	500 mL

Put garlic clove and oil in frying pan. Fry for about 1 minute or so depending on how strong you prefer it. Remove garlic and discard. Add bread cubes. Fry and stir until browned. Remove to plate. Cool before using in salad.

TOSSED SALAD

A good basic lettuce sure to please everyone. Onions for flavor and radishes for both color and flavor.

Lettuce, solid medium head	½	½
Green onions, sliced	3-5	3-5
Red radishes, sliced or chopped	4-5	4-5
Salad dressing to coat.		

Cut or tear lettuce into bite size pieces. Add onions and radishes. Serve with your favorite dressing.

TOSSED VEGETABLE SALAD: Add a bit of grated red cabbage to get color without a strong flavor. Add ½-1 green pepper, sliced or chopped along with 1-2 sticks of celery, sliced. A few slices of cucumber may also be added.

TOSSED MUSHROOM SALAD: Add ½-1 cup (125-250 mL) sliced fresh mushrooms to any variation of tossed salad. Adds more eye and taste appeal.

LETTUCE CROUTON TOSS: Add 1 tomato cut up and 1 cup (250 mL) croutons.

MOSTLY LETTUCE

If lettuce is the total of your salad makings, don't despair. Try this simple recipe.

Medium head lettuce (or leaf)	1	1
Cream, heavy or light	½ cup	125 mL
Granulated sugar	1 tsp.	5 mL

Cut or tear lettuce into salad bowl. Pour cream over top, sprinkle with sugar and toss to coat each piece.

LETTUCE ONION SALAD: Add a sprinkle of chives, dried or fresh, to above salad or 1-2 sliced green onions.

SOUR CREAM LETTUCE: Omit cream and sugar. Add 1 cup (250 mL) sour cream, 2 tbsp. (20 mL) granulated sugar, 1 tsp. (5 mL) salt and 2 tbsp. (30 mL) vinegar.

The Blue cheese gives just the right nip. Toss with a flair.

Clove of garlic, halved	1	1
Head of Romaine lettuce	1	1
Parmesan cheese	½ cup	125 mL
Blue cheese, crumbled	¼ cup	50 mL
Prepared mustard	1 tsp.	5 mL
Salt	¼ tsp.	1 mL
Pepper	⅛ tsp.	½ mL
Worcestershire sauce	1 tbsp.	15 mL
Wine vinegar or lemon juice	¼ cup	50 mL
Salad oil	⅓ cup	75 mL
Egg (Coddled — boiled 1 minute) optional	1	1
Croutons	2 cups	500 mL

Rub wooden salad bowl with cut side of garlic. Discard garlic. Tear lettuce into bite size pieces into bowl. Sprinkle with Parmesan cheese, Blue cheese, mustard, salt and pepper. Add Worcestershire sauce, vinegar and oil. Break coddled egg over top. Toss thoroughly to distribute and to coat every leaf.

Add croutons, toss quickly. Serves 8.

Note: If you would rather go the easy route, put lettuce, Parmesan and Blue cheese in salad bowl. Mix dressing (combine mustard, salt, pepper, Worcestershire, vinegar, oil and egg) separately. Pour over top. Toss, add croutons and toss again. Serve immediately.

CROUTONS: see page 13.

Paré Pointer

Ever feel like a doughnut? You're either in the dough or in the hole.

SECRET CAESAR

If you like to eat Caesar Salad without everyone else knowing that you did, this is for you.

DRESSING

Cooking oil	6 tbsp.	100 mL
Red wine vinegar	2 tbsp.	30 mL
Lemon juice	1 tbsp.	15 mL
Egg yolk	1	1
Worcestershire sauce	1 tsp.	5 mL
Garlic powder	¼ tsp.	1 mL
Salt	¼ tsp.	1 mL
Pepper	⅛ tsp.	½ mL
Grated Parmesan cheese	½ cup	125 mL

SALAD

Large head Romaine lettuce	1	1
Croutons	2 cups	500 mL
Parmesan cheese	¼ cup	50 mL

Combine all nine dressing ingredients in bowl. Mix together well. Set aside.

Tear lettuce into bite size pieces in salad bowl. Add croutons and cheese. Pour dressing over. Toss and serve. Serves 6.

CROUTONS: Add 2 cups (500 mL) plain dried croutons to frying pan with 2 tbsp. (30 mL) oil in it. Stir and fry. Sprinkle a little garlic salt over top. Fry until browned.

Caesar Salad page 19

This is it — a super, easy to make Caesar.

DRESSING

Garlic clove, mashed to a pulp	1	1
Egg yolk	1	1
Lemon juice	1 tbsp.	15 mL
Worcestershire sauce	1 tsp.	5 mL
Salad oil (or olive oil)	5 tbsp.	75 mL
Red wine vinegar	2 tbsp.	30 mL
Salt	¼ tsp.	1 mL
Pepper	⅛ tsp.	½ mL
Anchovies, chopped small	½ – 1 tin	½ – 1 tin
Grated Parmesan cheese	½ cup	125 mL

SALAD

Large head Romaine lettuce	1	1
Croutons	2 cups	500 mL
Grated Parmesan cheese	½ cup	125 mL

Make dressing in salad bowl by combining all ten dressing ingredients together. Mix together well.

Tear lettuce into bite size pieces in salad bowl. Toss to coat. Add croutons and Parmesan cheese and toss lightly once more. Serve immediately. Serves 6.

CROUTONS: Cut French bread into ½-¾ inch (1½-2 cm) cubes. Fry in garlic oil until browned.

GARLIC OIL: Slice 1 garlic clove into ½ cup (125 mL) olive oil or salad oil. Let stand for 4 hours. Discard garlic.

Note: Shrimp may be substituted in place of anchovies. Use fresh or tinned. Amount will vary depending on how many people you are serving.

Pictured on page 17.

Pare Pointer

A strong headed ruler is firm but a strong headed donkey is obstinate.

FOO YONG SUPREME

A Foo Yong Salad to end all Foo Yong Salads. Definitely the pick of them all. Prepare salad ahead but toss at the last moment.

DRESSING

Salad oil	¼ cup	50 mL
Granulated sugar	¼ cup	50 mL
Vinegar	2 tbsp.	30 mL
Ketchup	2⅔ tbsp.	40 mL
Grated onion	1 tbsp.	15 mL
Worcestershire sauce	1 tsp.	5 mL

Mix all ingredients together. Store in small covered bowl overnight if time permits.

SALAD

Large head Romaine lettuce	1	1
Bacon strips, cooked and crumbled	5	5
Generous handful bean sprouts (fresh is best)	1	1
Hard boiled eggs, chopped fine	2	2

Tear lettuce into bite size pieces. Sprinkle cold, crumbled bacon over top, then bean sprouts followed by chopped eggs. Can be prepared to this point, then refrigerated until the last minute. Pour all of the dressing over top. Toss together and serve at once. Serves 6.

Note: Head lettuce can be used instead of Romaine if you are preparing for a crowd. A large quantity can be cut up in no time. Add a portion of Romaine lettuce for looks.

COTTAGE GREENS

Quick and easy. Nice combination.

Cottage cheese	2 cups	500 mL
Shredded lettuce	2 cups	500 mL
Crushed pineapple, drained	14 oz.	398 mL
Salad dressing	2 tbsp.	30 mL

Put cottage cheese, lettuce and well drained pineapple in bowl.

Add salad dressing. Toss to mix well. Spoon into serving bowl. Serve.

Start with the basics and add as many or as few as desired. Have a different salad every day. Try several dressings.

Lettuce, solid medium head	1	1
Green onions, sliced	5-8	5-8
Red radishes, sliced or chopped	5-8	5-8
Red cabbage, sliced or shredded	½ cup	125 mL
Carrots, shredded	⅔ cup	150 mL
Small head cauliflower, separated	1	1
Medium Cheddar cheese, shredded or cubed	1 cup	250 mL
Blue Cheese, crumbled	¼ cup	50 mL
Avocado, sliced	1	1
Fresh mushrooms, sliced	1 cup	250 mL
Tomatoes, cut up	3-4	3-4
Celery, sliced diagonally	1½ cups	375 mL
Croutons	2 cups	500 mL
Green pepper, sliced	1	1
Red pepper, sliced	1	1
Cucumber, cut up	½	½
Salad dressing	½ cup	125 mL
Sour cream	½ cup	125 mL

Tear or cut salad greens into large bowl. Add the ingredients of your choice.

Mix salad dressing with sour cream, mixing more or less according to the amount of ingredients. Toss and serve.

Note: When taking a tossed salad to an event, it is better to serve the dressing on the side. A good mixture would be lettuce, green onion, large tomato chunks, celery, cucumber, mushrooms and green pepper. Cut green pepper in large enough pieces to be removed by those who don't care for it.

Paré Pointer

They wouldn't worry about what people think of them if they knew how seldom they do.

LETTUCE EGG TOSS

A superb additional way to serve lettuce. If eggs are in good supply, add another one or two.

Lettuce, solid medium head	½	½
Green onions, sliced (optional)	3-5	3-5
Hard boiled eggs, cut up	2	2
Salad dressing to coat		

Tear or cut lettuce into bite size pieces. Add onions and eggs. Add salad dressing. Toss and serve. Serves 6-8.

EGG MUSHROOM TOSS: Add ½-1 cup (125-250 mL) sliced fresh mushrooms before tossing.

LETTUCE CHEESE SALAD: Eggs may be omitted if preferred. Add ½-1 cup (125-250 mL) grated or diced medium Cheddar cheese. Colorful, healthy, good!

NO TOSS LETTUCE

Choose iceburg lettuce or Chinese cabbage.

Lettuce chunks or wedges	6 cups	1.5 L
Sliced green onions or		
thinly sliced onion rings	½ cup	125 mL

Arrange lettuce chunks on small size salad plates. Scatter onions over top. Spoon dressing over top and serve.

TARRAGON DRESSING

Sour cream	½ cup	125 mL
Tarragon vinegar	1 tbsp.	15 mL
Granulated sugar	2 tsp.	10 mL
Onion salt	½ tsp.	2 mL
Paprika	½ tsp.	2 mL

Combine all five ingredients together in small bowl. Mix well. Spoon over lettuce chunks.

Variation: Spoon French or Thousand Island dressing over lettuce wedges.

STUFFED TOMATOES

These are very showy salads. They can be stuffed with many fillings from coleslaw to meat. Different methods are described below.

TOMATO PREPARATION
Remove stem. Place stem end down. Cut vertical slices not quite to the bottom. Spread and stuff sandwich style. See "Note."

Remove stem. Place stem end down on counter. Cut about three quarters of the way down making a second, third and fourth cut so as to have eight sections. Spread apart and stuff. Tomato pulp may also be scooped out before stuffing. See "Note."

Remove stem. Place stem end on counter. Cut slices off the top — this will be the lid. Scoop out some of the pulp. Stuff with your favorite salad. Cover with top to form lid. Use small green pepper strip to make stem.

HAM STUFFING

Chopped ham	2 cups	500 mL
Chopped celery	1 cup	250 mL
Chopped cucumber	½ cup	125 mL
Chopped green onions	2	2
Mayonnaise	¼ cup	50 mL
Salt	¼ tsp	1 mL
Pinch of pepper		
Slivered almonds, toasted	1 tbsp.	15 mL

Combine first seven ingredients together. There should be enough to stuff 8 tomatoes. Sprinkle with almonds.

Note: Sprinkle inside of tomatoes with salt, then turn upside down to drain for a few minutes before filling if time permits.

Note: Toast almonds in 350°F (180°C) over for 5 minutes or until golden.

Pictured on page 35.

Too many committees waste hours and keep minutes.

GREEK SALAD

An old classic that is a meal in itself.

Head lettuce, torn bite size	½	½
Romaine lettuce	1	1
Tomatoes, cut bite size	2	2
Cucumber, cut bite size	1	1
Sliced green onions	¼ cup	50 mL
Sliced ripe olives	¼ cup	50 mL
Feta cheese, cubed	¾ cup	175 mL
Salad oil	½ cup	125 mL
Red wine vinegar	¼ cup	50 mL
Chopped parsley	¼ cup	50 mL
Salt	½ tsp.	2 mL
Pepper	⅛ tsp.	½ mL
Oregano	⅛ tsp.	½ mL
Garlic powder	⅛ tsp.	½ mL

Layer lettuce in large salad bowl or on large platter.

Spread with tomatoes, cucumber, onions, olives and cheese.

Beat next seven ingredients together well. Shake before serving. Serve with salad.

Note: A few sardines or anchovies may be arranged over top of salad. Feta cheese may be exchanged with 8 oz. (250 g) cream cheese, cubed.

CARROT RAISIN SALAD

A lunch box winner.

Shredded carrot	2 cups	500 mL
Raisins	½ cup	125 mL
Mayonnaise	⅓ cup	75 mL
Vinegar	1 tbsp.	15 mL

Put all ingredients into bowl. Toss to coat. Serves 6.

Note: If raisins are too dry, simmer covered in equal amount of water for 2 minutes. Let stand until cool. Drain. Pat dry with paper towel.

Variation: Add ½ cup (125 mL) chopped celery.

BEST VEGETABLE SALAD

And the best time-saving make-ahead. Delicious!

Sliced green beans, drained	14 oz.	398 mL
Kernel corn, drained	12 oz.	341 mL
Chopped green pepper	1 cup	250 mL
Sliced celery	1 cup	250 mL
Green onions, sliced	½ cup	125 mL
Diced pimento	2 tbsp.	30 mL
Granulated sugar	½ cup	125 mL
Cider vinegar	½ cup	125 mL
Salad oil	¼ cup	50 mL
Salt	½ tsp.	2 mL
Pepper	½ tsp.	2 mL

Measure first six vegetable ingredients in bowl.

Combine sugar, vinegar, oil, salt and pepper in small bowl. Stir until sugar is dissolved. Pour over vegetables. Toss to coat. Let stand overnight in refrigerator. Serves 10.

Note: Golden Caesar or Italian dressing compliments this salad exceptionally well.

FANCY RICE SALAD

Turn leftover rice into this yummy dish. Serve on lettuce with a roll.

Cold cooked rice	1 cup	250 mL
Crushed pineapple, drained	14 oz.	398 mL
Granulated sugar	¼ cup	50 mL
Whipping cream (or 1 envelope topping)	1 cup	250 mL
Mayonnaise	¼ cup	50 mL
Lettuce		
Maraschino cherries		

Combine rice, pineapple and sugar. Stir.

Whip cream until stiff. Beat in mayonnaise. Fold into rice mixture.

Arrange lettuce on plates. Spoon salad in center. Top with a cherry. Serve.

POTATO SALAD

A good all-round salad. Add extras if you wish.

Cooked potatoes, cubed, cold	6 cups	1.4 L
Hard boiled eggs		
(reserve slices) chopped	5	5
Chopped green onions	4	4
Chopped celery	½ cup	125 mL
Salad dressing	1 cup	250 mL
Milk	¼ cup	50 mL
Salt	1 tsp.	5 mL
Pepper	¼ tsp.	1 mL
Center egg slices (reserved)		
Tomato, cut up small	1	1
Salad dressing	3 tbsp.	50 mL
Milk	1 tbsp.	15 mL
Paprika for sprinkling		

Put potatoes in bowl. Reserve center slices of eggs equal to 2 eggs. Chop rest and add to potatoes along with onions and celery.

Mix salad dressing with milk, salt and pepper. Pour over potatoes. Pack into bowl. Smooth top.

Spread reserved egg slices over top of salad. Put chunks of tomato in spaces between egg slices. Mix salad dressing with milk. Drizzle over all trying to cover egg yolks so they don't dry. Sprinkle with paprika. Serves 8.

Variation: Several additions may be made such as radish, cucumber, lettuce, chopped pickle, more celery, green pepper.

Pictured on page 53.

Pare Pointer

She doesn't know much about common labor. She thinks a crowbar is where crows go to drink.

BEAN SPROUT SALAD

A touch of the orient. Delicious.

Bean sprouts	12 oz.	350 g
Green onions, sliced	¼ cup	50 mL
Salad oil (peanut or sesame is best)	2 tbsp.	30 mL
Soy sauce	2 tbsp.	30 mL
Sesame seeds toasted	2 tbsp.	30 mL
Granulated sugar	1 tbsp.	15 mL
Vinegar	1 tbsp.	15 mL
Pimento or red pepper strips	¼ cup	50 mL

Put bean sprouts and onions into bowl.

In small bowl combine salad oil, soy sauce, sesame seeds, sugar, vinegar and pimento. Stir to mix. Pour over sprouts and onions. Toss to coat. Serve.

Note: Toast sesame seeds in 350°F (180°C) oven for about 5 minutes until golden.

CUCUMBERS IN SOUR CREAM

A favorite that is one of the easiest.

Cucumbers, medium size	3	3
Salt	1½ tsp.	7 mL
Sour cream	1 cup	250 mL
Dry dill weed	½ tsp.	2 mL

Using a dinner fork, score clean cucumbers from top to bottom all round the outside. Slice thinly. Sprinkle with salt. Stir and allow to stand about ½ to 1 hour. Drain well.

Stir sour cream and dill together. Pour over cucumbers. Stir to cover all pieces. Serve. If time is short stir salt into sour cream and dill. Combine with cucumber just before serving to prevent cream from becoming too thin on standing. Serves 12-15.

Variation: Add 2 tbsp. (30 mL) lemon juice, 2 tbsp. (30 mL) parsley and 2 tbsp. (30 mL) granulated sugar.

BEAN SALAD

Colorful and tasty. You can double the onion rings to be sure to have enough to go around. Make days ahead.

Green beans, with juice	14 oz.	398 mL
Yellow wax beans, drained	14 oz.	398 mL
Lima beans, drained	14 oz.	398 mL
Kidney beans, drained	14 oz.	398 mL
Sliced onion rings	1 cup	250 mL
Sliced celery	1 cup	250 mL
Small can or jar pimento, chopped	1	1
Granulated sugar	1 cup	250 mL
Dry mustard	½ tsp.	3 mL
Salt	¼ tsp.	1 mL
Vinegar	1 cup	250 mL
Cooking oil	2 tbsp.	30 mL

Put green beans and juice into large bowl. Add drained yellow, lima and kidney beans. Slice onion rings about ¼ inch (¾ cm) thick. Add along with celery and pimento.

In another bowl, put sugar, mustard and salt. Stir together well. Add vinegar and oil. Stir until dissolved. It takes a few minutes. Pour over bean mixture. Cover and store in refrigerator. Let stand at least 24 hours before serving. Keeps for weeks. Dish up with a slotted spoon. Serves 25.

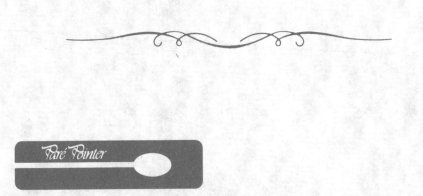

Santa Claus does his driving through the clouds because they hold rain, dear.

MARINATED ONION RINGS

These can be prepared days ahead. Just what you need for the barbeque feast. Perhaps you should double the recipe.

Large Spanish onion, sliced in thin rings	1	1
Cold water to cover		
Granulated sugar	1 cup	250 mL
Vinegar	1 cup	250 mL
Cold water	1 cup	250 mL
Salad oil	1 tbsp.	15 mL

Slice peeled onion into almost the thinnest slices you can. A food slicer makes this a snap to do. Separate into rings and place in bowl. Cover with lots of water. Let stand for 1 hour.

In small saucepan mix sugar, vinegar, water and oil. Heat and stir until sugar dissolves. Drain onions. Pour sugar-vinegar mixture over onions. Let stand in refrigerator, covered, for at least one day before serving. Serves 8-10.

WEEPY SALAD

The onions really do weep which helps moisten the whole salad.

Head lettuce in small chunks	1	1
Mayonnaise for a thin cover	½-1 cup	125-250 mL
Red onion (or white) sliced very thin	1	1
Granulated sugar	3 tsp.	15 mL
Cooked peas, fresh or frozen	1½ cups	375 mL
Swiss cheese cut in strips	1½ cups	375 mL
Bacon slices cooked and crumbled	6	6

Place one third lettuce chunks in bottom of bowl. Spread a few spoons of mayonnaise over top. Layer one third of thin onion slices over. Sprinkle lightly with sugar, about 1 tsp. (5 mL). Sugar all the onion as this causes them to weep. Put on one third of peas followed by one third cheese. Repeat layers twice. Cover and chill for 2-3 hours.

Before serving, sprinkle bacon over top. Do not toss.

JAPANESE CABBAGE SALAD

Out of the ordinary but worth the extra time. Cabbage blends in so well you scarcely know it is there. Most interesting texture. Try this for your next company.

Sliced or slivered almonds, toasted	½ cup	125 mL
Sesame seeds, toasted	2 tbsp.	30 mL
Medium cabbage, shredded	½ head	½ head
Bean sprouts	12 oz.	350 g
Fresh mushrooms, sliced	2 cups	500 mL
Green onions, chopped	2	2
Sunflower seeds	¼ cup	50 mL
Instant noodles, broken up (see Note)	3 oz. pkg.	85 g
Chow mein noodles	½ pkg.	½ pkg.

DRESSING

Seasoning from box of noodles	1 pkg.	1 pkg.
Cooking oil	½ cup	125 mL
Soy sauce	2-4 tbsp.	30-50 mL
Vinegar	3 tbsp.	45 mL
Granulated sugar	1 tbsp.	15 mL
Monosodium glutamate	1 tsp.	5 mL
Salt	1 tsp.	5 mL
Pepper	½ tsp.	2 mL

Put almonds and sesame seeds in single layer in pan. Toast in 350°F (180°C) oven for about 5 minutes (watch carefully as they can get too dark in no time) until golden. Remove from oven. Set aside.

Put shredded cabbage and bean sprouts into large bowl. Add mushrooms, onions and sunflower seeds. Add toasted almonds and sesame seeds.

Combine broken noodles and chow mein noodles in small bowl. Set aside.

(continued on next page)

DRESSING

Empty seasoning packet from box of noodles into small bowl. Add oil, lesser amount of soy sauce, vinegar and sugar. Add more soy sauce to taste. It will depend on quantity of cabbage. You will probably need full amount. Stir in monosodium glutamate, salt and pepper. Put in container with cover. Can be made ahead. Before serving, shake dressing. Pour over cabbage mixture. Toss. Sprinkle dry noodles over top followed by chow mein noodles.

JAPANESE SHRIMP SALAD: Add 2 cups (500 mL) canned or fresh cooked shrimp to cabbage mixture before tossing. Sliced cucumber and sliced radish may be added — about ½ cup (125 mL) of each.

ORIENTAL CHICKEN SALAD: Add 2 cups (500 mL) cooked chicken, cubed or cut in strips, to cabbage mixture before tossing. Sliced cucumber and sliced radish may be added — about ½ cup (125 mL) of each.

Note: Noodles come in 3 oz. (85 g) packages of instant noodles with chicken found in soup section of grocery stores. There are Japanese, Chinese and other brands as well.

VEGETABLE MARINADE

This serves not only as a salad but as an appetizer as well. Quantities are approximate and can be varied as can the vegetables.

Small cauliflower	1	1
Broccoli, flower ends	3 cups	750 mL
Cherry tomatoes	2 cups	500 mL
Celery, cut in sticks	2 cups	500 mL
Carrots, cut in sticks	3	3
Mushrooms, fresh or canned	2 cups	500 mL
Green pepper, cut in strips or rings	1	1
Italian dressing	1 cup	250 mL

Divide cauliflower into bite size pieces. Do the same with broccoli leaving some stem. Add tomatoes whole. Cut celery and carrots in sticks. Add mushrooms. Cut green pepper in strips or rings. Put into container with tight fitting cover. Pour Italian dressing over all. Put cover on. Shake to distribute dressing. Chill overnight turning container occasionally. Drain. Serve.

SAUERKRAUT SALAD

And there the similarity ends. Even if you don't like sauerkraut, you will love this tasty salad. Very attractive.

Sauerkraut	28 oz.	796 mL
Diced celery	1 cup	250 mL
Diced green pepper	1 cup	250 mL
Diced onion	¼ cup	50 mL
Small jar pimentos, chopped	1	1
Granulated sugar	¾ cup	175 mL
Salt	½ tsp.	3 mL
Pepper	⅛ tsp.	½ mL
Celery seed	1 tsp.	5 mL
Vinegar	3 tbsp.	50 mL

Drain sauerkraut. Rinse. Squeeze dry and chop. Put into large bowl.

Add rest of ingredients in order given. Mix together well. Let stand covered in refrigerator overnight before serving.

PENNY CARROTS

So versatile, this can be served cold as a salad or relish and also served hot. Try it hot over rice.

Carrots, sliced, cooked, drained	2 lbs.	1 kg
Condensed cream of tomato soup	10 oz.	284 mL
Granulated sugar	1 cup	250 mL
Vinegar	¾ cup	175 mL
Cooking oil	¼ cup	50 mL
Prepared mustard	1 tbsp.	15 mL
Medium onion, chopped	1	1
Green peppers, chopped	2	2

Slice carrots in ½ inch (1 cm) pieces. Cook. Drain.

Meanwhile combine soup with sugar in medium size saucepan. Add vinegar, oil, mustard, chopped onion and chopped peppers. Bring to boil stirring frequently. Pour over carrots. Chill covered for two days.

ONION SALAD

One of the best creamy good extras to serve.

Granulated sugar	½ cup	125 mL
Water	⅓ cup	75 mL
Vinegar (try cider)	⅓ cup	75 mL
Salt	1½ tsp.	7 mL
Spanish onions, sliced and cut	4	4
Mayonnaise	1 cup	250 mL
Celery seed	1 tsp.	5 mL

Put sugar, water, vinegar and salt into bowl. Stir until sugar dissolves.

Slice and cut onions. Add to vinegar mixture. Let stand for three hours or overnight.

Combine mayonnaise with celery seed. Drain onions well. Stir into mayonnaise. Serve.

GREEN PEA SALAD

Quick, colorful and tasty.

Cooked peas, fresh or frozen	2 cups	500 mL
Cheddar cheese, cubed	½ cup	125 mL
Salad dressing	1-4 tbsp.	15-60 mL
Salt sprinkle		
Pepper sprinkle		
Granulated sugar (optional, but good)		

Combine peas and cheese. Make sure peas are cold and well drained. Blot with paper towel to dry.

Start with a small amount of salad dressing, adding barely enough to coat. Mix in salt and pepper. Sprinkle with sugar to taste. Stir. Serves 4.

Variation: Add ½ cup (125 mL) chopped celery. One sliced green onion goes well too. Fresh sliced mushrooms make it special.

ORANGE ONION SALAD

Seems an unlikely combination, but it is delicious.

Large purple onion, sliced	1	1
Large oranges, sliced	2	2
Salad oil	¼ cup	50 mL
Lemon juice	1 tbsp.	15 mL
Salt	¼ tsp.	1 mL
Oregano	⅛ tsp.	½ mL
Lettuce leaves		
Ripe black olives, sliced (optional)	4	4

Slice onion thick. Soak in cold water ½ hour. Drain. Peel oranges. Slice crosswise into thin slices. Try for 8 onion slices and 12 orange slices.

Mix salad oil, lemon juice, salt and oregano together. Add onions and oranges. Marinate 15 minutes.

On four salad plates put lettuce leaves. Arrange 3 orange and 2 onion slices on top of each plate. Spoon a bit of marinade over top. Scatter olives over all. Serves 4.

Pictured on page 71.

ARTICHOKE SALAD: Add 14 oz. (398 mL) tin of drained artichoke heads. Toss.

Stuffed Tomatoes page 23

COLESLAW FOREVER

With this in the refrigerator you will never be caught short without a salad. Keeps and keeps and keeps.

Large cabbage, shredded	1	1
Medium carrots, grated	2	2
Medium onion, grated	1	1
Vinegar	¾ cup	175 mL
Salad oil	½ cup	125 mL
Granulated sugar	1½ cups	325 mL
Salt	1 tbsp.	15 mL
Celery seed	1 tbsp.	15 mL

Put cabbage, carrots and onion into large bowl.

Measure vinegar, oil, sugar, salt and celery seed into large saucepan. Bring to boil, stirring frequently. Pour hot over cabbage mixture. Stir to mix, pressing down until vegetables wilt and are covered with brine. Cool. Store in covered container in refrigerator. Let stand one or two days before eating. Keeps for weeks and weeks. Darkens a bit with age.

COTTAGE CHEESE SALAD

An easy mix of dairy and fresh garden produce.

Lettuce cups

Cottage cheese	2 cups	500 mL
Chopped radishes	¼ cup	50 mL
Sliced green onions or chives	2 tbsp.	30 mL
Mayonnaise (optional)	2 tbsp.	30 mL
Salt	1 tsp.	5 mL
Pepper	⅛ tsp.	½ mL

Paprika sprinkle

Arrange lettuce cups on one large or several small plates. A bowl may be used.

Combine cottage cheese, radishes, onions, mayonnaise, salt and pepper. Spoon into lettuce cups or bowl.

Sprinkle with paprika. Serve.

PARSNIP SALAD

You will have to try it to believe it.

Grated parsnips	1½ cups	375 mL
Chopped celery	½ cup	125 mL
Chopped green pepper	¼ cup	50 mL
Parsley flakes	½ tsp.	2 mL
Mayonnaise	⅓ cup	75 mL
Salad oil	1 tbsp.	15 mL
Vinegar	1 tbsp.	15 mL
Lemon juice	1 tsp.	5 mL
Salt	½ tsp.	2 mL

Combine parsnip, celery, green pepper and parsley in bowl.

Mix mayonnaise, salad oil, vinegar, lemon juice and salt together in measuring cup or bowl. Pour over parsnip mixture. Toss lightly. Serve.

MULTI LAYERED SALAD

There is only one word to describe this salad — amazing! Amazing how fresh it stays when made the day before. Read footnotes before making.

Medium head of lettuce with some spinach or Romaine mixed in	1	1
Sliced celery	1 cup	250 mL
Hard boiled eggs, chopped or sliced	6	6
Cooked peas, fresh or frozen	10 oz.	284 g
Chopped green pepper	½ cup	125 mL
Green onions, sliced	8	8
Water chestnuts, sliced thin	6 oz.	170 mL
Bacon slices, cooked and crumbled	8	8
Mayonnaise	1 cup	250 mL
Sour cream	1 cup	250 mL
Granulated sugar	2 tbsp.	30 mL
Cheddar cheese, grated	1 cup	250 mL
Bacon slices, cooked and crumbled	4	4

Cut or break lettuce into small pieces. Layer in bottom of 9 × 13 inch (22 × 33 cm) pan. Scatter each layer in order given.

Mix mayonnaise with sour cream and sugar. Spread over top being careful to seal right to the edge of pan.

(continued on next page)

Scatter grated cheese over followed by bacon. Seal well with plastic wrap. Store in refrigerator for at least 24 hours before serving. Cut into squares. Serves 10-12.

Notes: Depending on your likes, dislikes and possible allergies, several layers can be omitted. The most common layers are lettuce, eggs, peas, onions, bacon and mayonnaise.

LETTUCE: A mixture of greens is a good base.

PEAS: May be layered uncooked. Many do prefer raw.

BACON: May be used both as a layer and as a top garnish or may be used only as a layer or may be used only as a top garnish. Less bacon is needed when used only as a topping.

MAYONNAISE: Salad dressing may be used instead.

SOUR CREAM: Double the mayonnaise and omit sour cream if preferred.

CHEDDAR CHEESE: A lesser amount may be used for top garnish. Swiss cheese may be substituted. Also a heavy layer of Romano or Parmesan cheese may be substituted.

GARNISH: To have greens on top, sprinkle a few slices of green onion over all.

CONTAINER: A glass bowl shows off this salad. It makes the task of getting some of each layer a bit difficult.

FASTEST COLESLAW

Nothing to this after work. Buy shredded cabbage to save time.

Shredded cabbage	**4 cups**	**1 L**
Commercial coleslaw dressing	**¼ cup**	**50 mL**
Sprinkle of celery seeds		

Combine all together in bowl adding more dressing as needed. Toss and serve.

Variation: Add 1 tsp. (5 mL) dry onion flakes.

APPLE COLESLAW: Add ½ apple, grated and 1 small carrot, grated.

CABBAGE SALAD: Use grated cabbage only or add carrot, onion, whatever you like. For dressing use salad dressing with prepared mustard mixed in — enough for both color and taste. You may need a touch of sugar.

MID WEST COLESLAW

Nice creamy dressing, a bit more tart than some. Good.

Shredded cabbage	6 cups	1.4 L
Grated carrot	1	1
Minced onion	2 tbsp.	30 mL
Salad dressing	⅓ cup	75 mL
Salad oil	2 tbsp.	30 mL
Vinegar	1 tbsp.	15 mL
Celery seed	¼ tsp.	1 mL
Salt sprinkle		
Pepper sprinkle		

Combine cabbage, carrot and onion in salad bowl.

Mix next six ingredients together in small bowl. Add ¾ to cabbage mixture. Stir well adding more if needed. Serve.

CAULIFLOWER SALAD

When you want something different try this good dish.

Small cauliflower, grated	1	1
Green onions, sliced	3	3
Grated carrot	1	1
Salad dressing	½ cup	125 mL
Milk	1 tbsp.	15 mL
Salt	½ tsp.	2 mL

Grate cauliflower on medium or large grater. Combine in bowl with onions. Grate carrot on fine grater. Add.

Mix salad dressing, milk and salt together in measuring cup. Pour over cauliflower mixture. Toss lightly. Serve.

Time tells on a person — especially a good time.

SWEET POTATO SALAD

Now this really is different. Go ahead — try it.

Salad oil	2 tbsp.	30 mL
Pineapple juice	2 tbsp.	30 mL
Lemon juice	1 tbsp.	15 mL
Salt	½ tsp.	2 mL
Onion salt	¼ tsp.	1 mL
Cooked sweet potatoes, cubed	3 cups	700 mL
Pineapple bits, drained	14 oz.	398 mL
Chopped celery	¾ cup	175 mL
Slivered almonds	¼ cup	50 mL

Combine salad oil, pineapple and lemon juice in bowl. Add salt and onion salt. Stir. Add potato. Stir and allow to marinate about an hour.

Add pineapple, celery and almonds. Toss lightly. Serve.

QUICK COTTAGE CHEESE

The most simple way to serve cottage cheese and still make it attractive. No limit.

Cottage cheese
Paprika

Fill a pretty bowl with cottage cheese. Sprinkle with paprika. Serve.

One who thinks by the inch and talks by the yard needs to be moved by the foot.

MAIN MACARONI SALAD

A good, creamy main salad.

Macaroni or ready cut spaghetti	2 cups	500 mL
Chopped celery	¾ cup	175 mL
Sweet pickle relish	2 tbsp.	30 mL
Grated onion (or chopped green)	2 tbsp.	30 mL
Hard boiled eggs, chopped (optional)	2	2
Salad dressing	¾ cup	175 mL
Salt	1 tsp.	5 mL
Pepper	¼ tsp.	1 mL

Cook macaroni according to package directions. Drain very well. Cool.

Add celery, relish, onion, and chopped eggs.

In small bowl combine salad dressing, salt and pepper. Pour over salad. Stir. Chill. Radish garnish optional. Serves 6.

Pictured on page 53.

CARROT SALAD

Not only the young ones like this. Keeps well.

Shredded carrots	2 cups	500 mL
Green onions, sliced	2	2
Granulated sugar	4 tbsp.	60 mL
Vinegar	3 tbsp.	45 mL
Salad oil	1 tbsp.	15 mL
Salt	½ tsp.	2 mL
Pepper	¼ tsp.	1 mL
Lettuce		

Put carrot and onion in bowl.

Combine sugar, vinegar, salad oil, salt and pepper in small bowl. Stir to dissolve sugar. Pour over carrot mixture. Serve over lettuce.

FRUIT PLATTER

Fancy this up by using a melon baller if you wish. Especially good for breakfast or brunch entertaining. No sauce or dip is required for early in the day but later it is better to include them. Give thought to color before you decide what fruit to use. Also use a new fruit or melon for a change.

Cantaloupe, peeled, seeded, cut bite size
Honeydew, peeled, seeded, cut bite size
Watermelon, peeled, seeded, cut bite size
Strawberries, left whole
Bananas, peeled, cut dipped in orange juice
Kiwi fruit, peeled, sliced
Apples, unpeeled, cut in wedges, dipped in orange juice
Green grapes
Red grapes
Oranges, peeled, cut in wedges
Ripe pineapple, cut in chunks or spears
Papaya, peeled, seeded, cut bite size

And of course there are many more in season. Pile fruit in separate sections on tray. It can also be piled in rows. Or if you prefer, fruit can be mixed all together. Let guests help themselves. If served in a dish, serve fruit sauce on the side. If served as a finger food, have a dip or two nearby. Try to serve a minimum of 3 or 4 varieties.

Pictured on page 71.

JELLY POWDER SALAD

A different, tasty salad. Try other gelatin flavors as well.

Whipping cream (or 1 envelope topping)	1 cup	250 mL
Cottage cheese	1 cup	250 mL
Crushed pineapple, drained	14 oz.	398 mL
Dry lime-flavored gelatin	1 – 3 oz.	1 – 85 g
Fruit cocktail, drained	2 – 14 oz.	2 – 398 mL
Chopped pecans or walnuts	½ cup	125 mL

Whip cream until stiff.

Fold in cottage cheese, pineapple, dry jelly powder, fruit cocktail and nuts. Chill overnight.

COTTAGE FRUIT SALAD

Makes a good breakfast or brunch salad.

Cottage cheese	2 cups	500 mL
Salad dressing	¼ cup	50 mL
Crushed pineapple, well drained	14 oz.	398 mL
Diced unpeeled apple	1	1
Chopped pecans or walnuts	½ cup	125 mL

Lettuce cups
Unpeeled apple slices dipped in
   lemon juice
Maraschino cherries

Put cottage cheese into bowl. Stir in salad dressing. Add drained pineapple, apple and nuts. Stir.

Scoop into lettuce cups. Arrange apple slices around sides. Top with cherry.

Variation: Add ½ cup (125 mL) raisins. Diced apple may be omitted or left in salad.

SOFT FRUIT SALAD

Definitely an in-season salad. Try it when ingredients permit.

Bananas, peeled and sliced	2	2
Papaya, peeled and sliced	1	1
Mango, peeled and chunked	1	1
Kiwi fruit, peeled and sliced	2	2
Orange, sectioned or sliced	1	1
Sliced almonds, toasted	½ cup	125 mL
Maraschino cherry juice	2 tbsp.	30 mL
Vinegar	1 tbsp.	15 mL
Salad oil	1 tbsp.	15 mL
Granulated sugar	2 tbsp.	30 mL

Combine all fruit in bowl.

Put almonds, cherry juice, vinegar, salad oil and sugar in small bowl. Stir. Pour over fruit. Serve.

Note: Toast almonds in 350°F (180°C) oven for 5 minutes until golden.

TWENTY FOUR HOUR SALAD

A delicious salad, fruity and creamy.

Eggs	2	2
Granulated sugar	2 tbsp.	30 mL
Vinegar	2 tbsp.	30 mL
Pineapple juice	2 tbsp.	30 mL
Butter or margarine	1 tbsp.	15 mL
Pinch of salt		
Fruit cocktail, drained	14 oz.	398 mL
Pineapple pieces, drained	14 oz.	398 mL
Seedless grapes, halved, optional	½ cup	125 mL
Banana sliced	1	1
Small marshmallows	2 cups	500 mL
Whipping cream (or 1 envelope topping)	1 cup	250 mL

Beat eggs with spoon in top of double boiler. Stir in sugar, vinegar, pineapple juice, butter and salt. Cook and stir over boiling water until thickened. Chill thoroughly.

Add well drained fruit cocktail and pineapple to egg mixture. Add grapes, banana and marshmallows.

Whip cream until stiff. Fold into fruit. Chill overnight for twenty four hours.

FIVE CUP SALAD

A great make-from-the shelf salad. Quick, easy and tasty.

Orange segments, drained	10 oz.	284 mL
Pineapple pieces, drained	14 oz.	398 mL
Coconut, medium or shredded	1 cup	250 mL
Marshmallows	1 cup	250 mL
Sour cream	1 cup	250 mL
Red maraschino cherries, whole or halved (optional)	6-10	6-10

Put all ingredients into bowl. Stir gently until well mixed. Turn into serving dish. Decorate with cherries or mix the cherries in. Serves 6-8.

SPRING SALAD

Takes just minutes to prepare this fruit everyone enjoys.

Lettuce cups

Orange sections, drained (or fresh)	**10 oz.**	**284 g**
Bananas, sliced	**2**	**2**
Red grapes, halved, seeded	**24**	**24**
Mayonnaise	**¼ cup**	**50 mL**
Whipping cream		
(whipped), or topping	**¼ cup**	**50 mL**
Raisins	**⅓ cup**	**75 mL**
Chopped walnuts or pecans (optional)		

Put lettuce on 4-6 plates.

Arrange orange sections, banana and grapes on lettuce. Dip banana in orange juice to keep from darkening.

Fold mayonnaise into whipped cream. Spoon over top of salads.

Sprinkle with raisins and also with nuts if you are using them. Serves 4-6.

Pictured on page 71.

BANANA SALAD

Bring the tropics to the table. The kids love it.

Bananas	**3**	**3**
Finely chopped nuts	**½ cup**	**125 mL**
Lettuce leaves		
Whipping cream		
(or 1 envelope topping)	**¼ cup**	**50 mL**
Mayonnaise	**¼ cup**	**50 mL**

Cut bananas in half crosswise, then in half again lengthwise. Dip each piece in lemon juice. Roll in nuts and arrange on lettuce leaves. This can be done on one large plate or on individual small plates.

Whip cream until stiff. Mix in mayonnaise. Spoon over bananas.

Variation: Omit nuts. Roll in toasted coconut.

SMALL SALAD

Enough for one serving. Simple to increase.

Lettuce leaf (or shredded)	1	1
Pear or peach half	1	1
Cottage cheese	2-3 tbsp.	30-45 mL
Paprika sprinkle		

Put lettuce leaf on plate. Place pear or peach half flat side up. Spoon scoop of cottage cheese in center. Sprinkle paprika over top. Serves 1.

SMALLER SALAD

A single serving which can easily be multiplied.

Lettuce leaf (or shredded)	1	1
Pear or peach half	1	1
Mayonnaise		
Cheddar cheese, shredded for sprinkling		

Put lettuce leaf on plate. Place pear or peach half flat side up. Spoon dollop of mayonnaise in center. Sprinkle with cheese. Serves 1.

OLD FASHIONED WALDORF

Just as good now as way back then. Dressing is delicious.

Peeled apple, diced	1 cup	250 mL
Chopped celery	1 cup	250 mL
Red grapes, halved and seeded	½ cup	125 mL
Chopped walnuts	½ cup	125 mL
DRESSING		
Whipping cream	1 cup	250 mL
Granulated sugar	¼ cup	50 mL
Vinegar	3 tbsp.	45 mL

Combine apples, celery, grapes and nuts. Stir.

Whip cream until almost stiff. Add sugar. Beat in vinegar slowly. Pour over apple. Fold together. Serves 4.

BANANA PEANUT BUTTER SALAD

The young ones are keen about this salad. Good in lunch boxes or for snacks.

Bananas	2-3	2-3
Smooth peanut butter for spreading		
Orange juice for dipping		
Mayonnaise		

Cut bananas in half crosswise, then in half lengthwise. Spread peanut butter between matching halves. Stick together. Dip each sandwiched half in orange juice (or use lemon juice). Serve with a small dollop of mayonnaise over each.

SAUCED BANANAS

Prepare bananas with peanut butter. Omit mayonnaise.

Vinegar	½ cup	125 mL
Water	½ cup	125 mL
Egg, beaten	1	1
Granulated sugar	½ cup	125 mL
All purpose flour	1 tbsp.	15 mL
Salt	⅛ tsp.	½ mL

Bring vinegar and water to boil in saucepan.

Mix beaten egg with sugar, flour and salt. Stir into hot liquid. Stir until it boils and is thickened. Pour over bananas and serve.

FRUIT SNACK

This is just the thing when appetites call for something light. Make it right from the shelf, add toast or muffins and your snack is complete.

Pineapple chunks, drained	14 oz.	398 mL
Canned oranges, drained	10 oz.	284 mL
Bananas, sliced	2	2

Combine pineapple, oranges and bananas together in bowl. Spoon on a bit of the pineapple juice or serve it in separate container. Serves 2-3.

PISTACHIO SALAD

Such a treat to eat. So different. Try it spooned over fresh fruit too.

Pistachio instant pudding powder (4 portion size)	1	1
Milk	1¾ cup	400 mL
Crushed pineapple, well drained	14 oz.	398 mL
Small marshmallows	2 cups	500 mL
Chopped nuts (optional but good)	½ cup	125 mL
Whipping cream (or 1 envelope topping)	1 cup	250 mL
Lettuce, cups or shredded		

In medium bowl mix pudding powder with milk.
Add well drained pineapple along with marshmallows and nuts.

Whip cream until stiff. Fold into pudding mixture. Chill. Serve over lettuce.

Variation: Use pineapple juice and omit milk. Makes a more solid but less smooth salad.

INSTANT FRUIT SALAD: Use vanilla instant pudding instead of pistachio. Omit milk and pineapple. Add 1 tin fruit cocktail with juice, 14 oz. (398 mL). Makes quite a different salad.

PEACH PIE SALAD

An unusual way to begin a salad. It is so good.

Peach pie filling	19 oz.	540 mL
Pineapple pieces, drained	14 oz.	398 mL
Fruit cocktail, drained	14 oz.	398 mL
Sliced bananas	2	2
Seedless green grapes	1 cup	250 mL
Small marshmallows	1 cup	250 mL

Put pie filling into bowl. Stir in drained pineapple and drained fruit cocktail. Add sliced bananas. Add grapes and marshmallows. Stir together. Turn into a pretty serving bowl and chill several hours before serving.

WALDORF ORIGINAL

Although the original salad of the Waldorf Astoria Hotel is reported not to contain nuts, it has become a natural ingredient.

Peeled apple, diced	1 cup	250 mL
Chopped celery	1 cup	250 mL
Chopped walnuts	½ cup	125 mL
Mayonnaise	¼ cup	50 mL
Lemon juice	2 tbsp.	30 mL

Put apple, celery and walnuts into bowl.

Add mayonnaise and lemon juice immediately to prevent apple from darkening. Serves 4.

Variation: Try with thousand island dressing or with French dressing rather than mayonnaise and lemon juice.

Variation: Use only half as much celery. Add ½ cup (125 mL) cheese croutons just before serving.

Variation: Omit mayonnaise and lemon juice. Add ¼ cup (50 mL) salad dressing.

ORANGE FRUIT SALAD

A speedy salad compiled from the kitchen shelf.

Lettuce leaves	6	6
Whipping cream **(or 1 envelope topping)**	1 cup	250 mL
Salad dressing	¼ cup	50 mL
Fruit cocktail, well drained	14 oz.	398 mL
Orange segments, drained **(reserve 18 for garnish)**	10 oz.	284 mL

Arrange lettuce leaves like a cup on 6 plates.

Whip cream until stiff. Fold in salad dressing.

Add fruit cocktail and orange segments. Pile on lettuce leaves. Put 3 orange sections fan shape on top of each serving. Serves 6.

FRUIT COMBO SALAD

When fresh peaches are available, try this combination.

DRESSING

Granulated sugar	½ cup	125 mL
Corn starch	2 tsp.	10 mL
Orange juice	1 cup	250 mL
Peaches, peeled and sliced	2	2
Apples, unpeeled and diced	2	2
Oranges, peeled and sectioned	2	2
Bananas, sliced	2	2

Combine sugar and corn starch in saucepan. Mix well. Stir in orange juice. Cook and stir over medium heat until it boils and is thickened. Remove from heat. Cool.

Stir fruit together in bowl. Apples can be sliced if preferred. Serve with cooled orange dressing.

HAWAIIAN SALAD

This can serve as many or as few as desired. Picturesque.

Lettuce cups (or shredded)	1	1
Pineapple rings	2	2
Banana slices, scored	4-6	4-6
Macadamia nuts	1 tbsp.	15 mL

Place lettuce on plate. Lay pineapple rings, overlapping, on lettuce. Score peeled banana with fork. Cut slices diagonally and layer overlapping on top of pineapple after first dipping them in pineapple juice. Sprinkle nuts over top. Serves 1.

Note: A touch of mayonnaise or sour cream would make a topping if desired.

PINEAPPLE BOAT SALAD

A refreshing tropical island luncheon. Garnish with greens and perhaps a flower.

Ripe pineapple, cut lengthwise	**2**	**2**
Strawberries, halved	**2 cups**	**500 mL**
Pineapple pieces	**2 cups**	**500 mL**
Seedless green grapes, halved	**½ cup**	**125 mL**
Purple grapes, halved and seeded	**½ cup**	**125 mL**
Kiwi fruit, peeled and sliced	**1**	**1**
Bananas, sliced	**2**	**2**
Cottage cheese	**2 cups**	**500 mL**
Chopped pecans or walnuts	**½ cup**	**125 mL**
Chopped green onion	**1**	**1**
Nuts for sprinkling		

Cut pineapples lengthwise keeping leaves attached. Remove core and scoop out pineapple. Cut in pieces. You probably won't need all of the pineapple chunks.

Divide next six fruit ingredients among four pineapple boats.

Mix cottage cheese, first ½ cup (125 mL), nuts and onion together. Put 3 scoops on top of each fruit filled boat.

Sprinkle with nuts. Serves 4.

PINEAPPLE CANOES: Cut pineapple into 4 lengthwise sections keeping leaves on each. Makes 8 smaller servings.

1. Potato Salad page 26
2. Main Macaroni Salad page 42

ORANGE ALMOND SALAD

Pretty, nutty and delicious. Men like this as well.

Romaine lettuce	1	1
Orange segments, drained	10 oz.	284 mL
Green onions, sliced	2	2
Slivered almonds, toasted	¼ cup	50 mL
Salad oil	¼ cup	50 mL
Vinegar	¼ cup	50 mL
Granulated sugar	¼ cup	50 mL

Tear lettuce into bite size pieces. Arrange over salad plates. Divide orange sections over lettuce. Scatter green onions over top. Sprinkle with almonds.

Stir salad oil, vinegar and sugar together well. Pour over salad. Serve. Makes 4-6 servings.

Note: Toast almonds in pan in 350°F (180°C) oven for about 5 minutes until golden.

FRESH FRUIT SALAD

One of the most popular salads going. Try the variations too.

Fresh pineapple, cut bite size	½	½
Oranges, peeled and sectioned	2	2
Grapefruit, peeled and sectioned	1	1
Bananas, cut in thick slices	2	2
Lettuce		
Cottage cheese	1 cup	250 mL
Maraschino cherries	4	4

Arrange fruit in four individual salad bowls lined with lettuce.

Top with scoops of cottage cheese and top with cherries.

Variation: Add apple wedges.

Variation: Add bananas split and spread with peanut butter.

Variation: Omit cottage cheese. Top with scoops of ice cream.

CANTALOUPE MOLD

Put out a surprise for lunch.

Red or orange-flavored gelatin	1 – 3 oz.	1 – 85 g
Boiling water	1 cup	250 mL
Cold water	1 cup	200 mL
Cantaloupes	2	2
Salad dressing or mayonnaise		

Dissolve gelatin in boiling water. Stir in cold water. Chill until syrupy.

Cut cantaloupe in half. Scoop out seeds. Remove enough fruit to leave shell about ½ inch (1⅛ cm) thick. Chop removed fruit. Drain. Fold into thickened jelly. Spoon into cantaloupe halves. Chill until firm.

To serve, cut each half in half. Top with salad dressing. Serves 8.

Variation: Well drained fruit cocktail may be added to make it more fruity. Combining salad dressing with whipped cream is also a good topping.

FRESH CRANBERRY SALAD

This must be the fanciest way to eat cranberries.

Cranberries, fresh or frozen, ground	2 cups	500 mL
Medium apple, unpeeled and cubed	1	1
Crushed pineapple, drained	14 oz.	398 mL
Granulated sugar	¾ cup	175 mL
Small marshmallows	2 cups	500 mL
Whipping cream (or 1 envelope topping)	1 cup	250 mL
Lettuce cups or leaves		
Finely chopped pecans or walnuts	¼ cup	50 mL

Stir ground cranberries and diced apple together in bowl. Add drained pineapple, sugar and marshmallows.

Whip cream until stiff. Fold into cranberry mixture and chill until ready to serve. Heap in lettuce cups. Sprinkle with nuts before serving.

EVENING FRUIT SALAD

Keep supplies on hand and make this at a moments notice.

Fruit cocktail, drained	14 oz.	398 mL
Orange sections, drained	10 oz.	284 mL
Sliced banana	1	1
Purple grapes, halved and seeded	10	10
Small marshmallows	2 cups	500 mL
Whipping cream (or 1 envelope topping)	1 cup	250 mL
Chopped pecans or walnuts	½ cup	125 mL

Drain fruit very well. Reserve some orange segments for topping. Combine drained fruit with banana, grapes and marshmallows.

Whip cream until stiff. Fold in nuts. Fold into fruit. Serve from serving bowl or in lettuce cups. Top with reserved orange segments.

STUFFED APRICOT SALAD

Serve one or ten. You decide. Very attractive.

Lettuce cup (or shredded lettuce)	1	1
Apricot halves (fresh is best)	4-6	4-6
Cream cheese, softened	4 tbsp.	60 mL
Cream or milk	1 tsp.	5 mL
Dates, chopped fine	2 tbsp.	30 mL

Place lettuce on plate. Arrange apricot halves on top. Mash cheese and milk adding two thirds of the dates. Spoon into center of apricots. Sprinkle rest of dates over top. Serves 1.

Pare Pointer

Most of us get experience when we are really looking for something else.

HAM SALAD MATE

This is the perfect salad mate to serve with ham. Can be made the day before.

Eggs	4	4
Water	1 cup	225 mL
Cider vinegar	½ cup	110 mL
Granulated sugar	¾ cup	175 mL
Unflavored gelatin powder	¼ oz.	7 g
Turmeric	½ tsp.	2 mL
Salt	¼ tsp.	1 mL
Dry mustard powder	1½ tbsp.	20 mL
Whipping cream (or 1 envelope topping)	1 cup	250 mL

Beat eggs together well in top of double boiler. Stir in water and vinegar. Set aside.

Measure sugar into medium size bowl. Add gelatin, tumeric, salt and mustard powder. Stir all together until thoroughly mixed. Add to egg mixture and mix. Place over boiling water. Cook and stir until thickened slightly. Remove from heat and cool until mixture is syrupy thick.

Beat cream until stiff. Fold into thickened jelly. Then pour into 1½ quart (1½ L) mold. Chill several hours.

LEMON SATIN SALAD

Cuts into soft squares for easy serving. Refreshing taste.

Unflavored gelatin powders	2 – ¼ oz.	2 – 7 g
Cold water	½ cup	125 mL
Lemon juice	½ cup	125 mL
Salad dressing	1 cup	225 mL
Milk	½ cup	125 mL
Instant lemon pudding powder	1 – 3½ oz.	1 – 92 g

Sprinkle gelatin powders over cold water and lemon juice in small saucepan. Let stand for 5 minutes to soften. Heat and stir over medium heat to dissolve. Chill until syrupy.

Put salad dressing, milk and pudding powder in medium bowl. Add thickened gelatin. Stir together well. Pour into loaf pan or mold. Chill.

A mild version of a Spanish specialty.

Unflavored gelatin powders	2 – ¼ oz.	2 – 7 g
Cold water	½ cup	125 mL
Beef bouillon cube	1	1
Canned tomatoes with juice	14 oz.	398 mL
Unpeeled cucumber, diced	½ cup	125 mL
Diced green pepper	¼ cup	50 mL
Chopped celery	¼ cup	50 mL
Green onions, sliced	3	3
Vinegar	3 tbsp.	45 mL
Salt	¼ tsp.	1 mL
Garlic powder	⅛ tsp.	½ mL
Sour cream for garnish		

Sprinkle gelatin powder over water in small saucepan. Let stand 5 minutes to soften. Heat and stir over low heat to dissolve gelatin.

Add bouillon cube. Stir until dissolved. Remove from heat.

Add next eight ingredients, cutting up any tomato chunks. Stir. Chill until syrupy. Pour into mold or bowl. Chill.

Serve with dollop of sour cream.

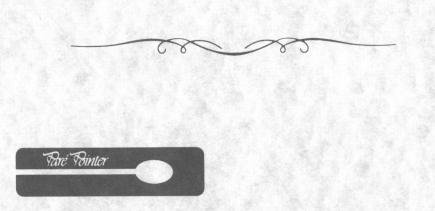

Pare Pointer

Don't expect too much from the man who talks about what he did instead of what he's doing.

APRICOT CREAM SALAD

A refreshing bit of fluff. Serve as is or scoop over fruit salad.

Unflavored gelatin powder	1 – ¼ oz.	1 – 7g
Cold water	¼ cup	50 mL
Juice from apricots		
(add water if needed)	1 cup	225 mL
Apricots, drained and puréed	14 oz.	398 mL
Granulated sugar	¼ cup	50 mL
Whipping cream		
(or 1 envelope topping)	1 cup	250 mL

Sprinkle gelatin over water in small saucepan. Let stand 5 minutes to soften.

Add juice and water. Heat and stir over medium heat to dissolve gelatin. Stir in apricots and sugar. Remove from heat. Chill until syrupy.

Whip cream until stiff. Fold into thickened gelatin. Pour into mold or serving bowl. Chill.

DOUBLE CHEESE MOLD

A delicious salad. It is one salad men really like.

Unflavored gelatin powders	2 – ¼ oz.	2 – 7 g
Cold water	1½ cups	350 mL
Cream cheese, softened	2 – 8 oz.	2 – 250 g
Medium Cheddar cheese, grated	2 cups	500 mL
Minced onion	1 tbsp.	15 mL
Worcestershire sauce	2 tsp.	10 mL
Lemon juice	2 tsp.	10 mL
Pinch of salt		
Pinch of cayenne		

Sprinkle gelatin over water in saucepan. Let stand 5 minutes. Then heat and stir over low heat until dissolved. Remove from heat.

Mash softened cream cheese on large plate until soft. Add grated Cheddar. Mash together until combined. Add onion, Worcestershire sauce, lemon juice, salt and cayenne. Mix together well. Scrape into gelatin. Stir or whisk until blended. Turn into mold or glass bowl. Chill.

Try a Spanish favorite. Good with any meat.

Unflavored gelatin powders	2 – ¼ oz.	2 – 7 g
Cold water	½ cup	125 mL
Tomato juice	1¼ cups	275 mL
Red wine vinegar	⅓ cup	75 mL
Salt	1 tsp.	5 mL
Tabasco sauce, drops	1-4	1-4
Diced tomatoes (preferably peeled)	2	2
Peeled cucumber, diced	1	1
Green pepper, diced	½	½
Chopped onion	¼ cup	50 mL
Chopped chives	1 tbsp.	15 mL

Sour cream for garnish

Sprinkle gelatin over water in small saucepan. Let stand 5 minutes to soften. Then heat and stir over medium heat to dissolve gelatin.

Add tomato juice, vinegar and salt. Add tomatoes, cucumber, green pepper, onion and chives. Chill, stirring once or twice until syrupy. Pour into mold or bowl. Chill.

To serve, top with a dollop of sour cream.

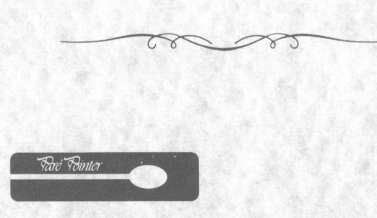

Paré Pointer

A worker who spends most of the time watching the clock usually remains one of the hands.

PERFECTION SALAD

One of the better known, and one of the best.

Unflavored gelatin powder	1 – ¼ oz.	1 – 7 g
Granulated sugar	¼ cup	50 mL
Salt	½ tsp.	2 mL
Boiling water	¾ cup	175 mL
Cold water	½ cup	125 mL
Vinegar	¼ cup	50 mL
Lemon juice	2 tbsp.	30 mL
Shredded cabbage	⅔ cup	150 mL
Chopped celery	½ cup	125 mL
Cooked peas, fresh or frozen	⅓ cup	75 mL
Green pepper, diced	¼ cup	50 mL
Chopped pimento	2 tbsp.	30 mL

Mix gelatin powder, sugar and salt together very well in bowl.

Add boiling water. Stir to dissolve. Stir in cold water, vinegar and lemon juice. Chill until syrupy.

Add cabbage, celery, peas, green pepper and pimento to thickened gelatin. Turn into mold or serving bowl. Chill.

BLUE CHEESE MOLD

Put a little nip in your menu.

Unflavored gelatin powder	1 – ¼ oz.	1 – 7 g
Cold water	¼ cup	50 mL
Boiling water	¾ cup	175 mL
Cream cheese, slivered	8 oz.	250 g
Blue cheese, crumbled	4 oz.	113 g
Cottage cheese	1 cup	225 mL
Onion salt	¼ tsp.	1 mL
Celery salt	⅛ tsp.	½ mL
Paprika	⅛ tsp.	½ mL

Sprinkle gelatin over ¼ cup water. Let stand 5 minutes. Add boiling water. Stir to dissolve.

Using cheese wire cutter or paring knife, cut small pieces of cream cheese into gelatin. Stir in remaining five ingredients. Pour into mold. Chill. Serves 8-10.

STRAWBERRY LAYERED SALAD

Makes a shiny red top mold with a creamy pink base. As good as it looks. Nutty flavor.

Stawberry-flavored gelatin	2–3 oz.	2–85 g
Boiling water	1 cup	225 mL
Frozen strawberries, thawed	2 – 15 oz.	2 – 425 g
Crushed pineapple and juice	14 oz.	398 mL
Bananas, mashed	3	3
Chopped walnuts	1 cup	225 g
Sour cream	1 cup	225 mL

Dissolve gelatin in boiling water.

Add strawberries, pineapple, mashed bananas and nuts. Chill until syrupy. Pour half of the jelly into mold. Chill. Leave second half at room temperature.

Stir sour cream in second half of jelly. Pour over almost firm jelly in mold. Chill.

STRAWBERRY CREAM

So attractive to serve. Nice and fruity.

Stawberry-flavored gelatin	1 – 3 oz.	1 – 85 g
Boiling water	1 cup	225 mL
Strawberry juice plus enough pineapple juice to make	¾ cup	175 mL
Frozen strawberries, thawed and drained	½ of 15 oz.	½ of 425 g
Crushed pineapple, drained	14 oz.	498 mL
Banana, diced	1	1
Sour cream	1 cup	225 mL

Dissolve gelatin in boiling water in bowl. Stir in juice.

Add strawberries and pineapple. Stir in diced banana. Pour half into 8 x 8 inch (20 x 20 cm) pan. Chill until firm. Chill second half until it begins to thicken.

Spread sour cream over firm jelly in pan. Spoon thickened jelly (second half) over top. Chill. Cut in squares to serve. Makes 9 pieces.

CHERRY CHEESE SALAD

Just right for a bridal shower, a ladies meeting or a club get-together.
Serve with parkerhouse rolls. A creamy lemon top layer over a red base.

Raspberry-flavored gelatin	1 – 3 oz.	1 – 85 g
Boiling water	1 cup	225 mL
Cherry pie filling	19 oz.	540 mL
Lemon-flavored gelatin	1 – 3 oz.	1 – 85 g
Boiling water	1 cup	225 mL
Cream cheese	4 oz.	125 g
Mayonnaise	⅓ cup	75 mL
Crushed pineapple with juice	1 cup	225 mL
Whipping cream		
(or 1 envelope topping)	1 cup	250 mL
Small white marshmallows	1½ cups	375 mL
Chopped nuts	2 tbsp.	30 mL
Lettuce		

Dissolve raspberry gelatin in boiling water. Stir in pie fiing. Pour into 9 x 9 inch (22 x 22 cm) pan. Chill until almost set then pour on next layer.

Dissolve lemon gelatin in boiling water. Set aside.

Have cream cheese at room temperature. Beat cheese and mayonnaise together in small bowl. Mix in dissolved lemon gelatin. Stir in pineapple with juice. Chill until syrupy.

Whip cream until stiff. Fold into lemon gelatin. Add marshmallows and fold in. Pour over cherry layer. Sprinkle nuts over top. Chill.

Serve on shredded or leaf lettuce. Cuts into 9 or 12 thick portions.

Pare Pointer

Life is a measure to be filled and not a cup to empty.

Served on a lettuce leaf, this outshines most salads.

Raspberry-flavored gelatin	1 – 3 oz.	1 – 85 g
Boiling water	1 cup	225 mL
Frozen raspberries, almost thawed	10 oz.	284 g
Lemon-flavored gelatin	1 – 3 oz.	1 – 85 g
Boiling water	1 cup	225 mL
Crushed pineapple with juice	1 cup	225 mL
Cream cheese, slivered in	4 oz.	125 g
Whipping cream	1 cup	250 mL
Lime-flavored gelatin	1 – 3 oz.	1 – 85 g
Boiling water	1¼ cup	275 mL
Crushed pineapple with juice	1 cup	225 mL

Dissolve raspberry gelatin in boiling water. Stir in raspberries. Pour into 9 × 9 inch (22 × 22 cm) pan. Chill until firm.

Dissolve lemon gelatin in boiling water. Stir in pineapple. Slice cheese in. Chill until syrupy. Whip cream until stiff. Fold into thickened jelly. Spoon over firm red layer. Chill until firm.

Dissolve lime gelatin in boiling water. Stir in pineapple. Chill until quite syrupy. Spoon over firm yellow layer. Chill until firm. Cut into squares to serve.

RIBBON PASTEL SALAD: Whip 1 cup (250 mL) cream for each of red and green layers. Fold into thickened jelly. Sprinkle top with chopped nuts. Gives the salad a soft appearance.

SIMPLE RIBBON SALAD: For red layer omit raspberries. Use 2 cups (450 mL) water. For yellow layer omit cream cheese. For green layer omit pineapple. Use 2 cups (450 mL) water. Makes a pretty salad which is very economical.

Paré Pointer

Quit worrying about hating your job so much. Someone else will have it soon.

FESTIVE EGGNOG SALAD

But it has no eggnog in it! Festive is the word and it does taste like eggnog. A beautiful red base topped with a yellow crown.

Vanilla pudding mix (not instant), 4 portion size	1	1
Lemon-flavored gelatin	1 – 3 oz.	1 – 85 g
Water	2 cups	450 mL
Lemon juice	2 tbsp.	30 mL
Raspberry-flavored gelatin	1 – 3 oz.	1 – 85 g
Boiling water	1 cup	225 mL
Whole cranberry sauce	2 cups	450 mL
Celery, finely chopped	½ cup	125 mL
Pecans or walnuts, finely chopped	⅓ cup	75 mL
Whipping cream (or 1 envelope topping)	1 cup	250 mL
Nutmeg	½ tsp.	2 mL

Put pudding mix and lemon gelatin in medium size saucepan. Gradually stir in water and lemon juice. Cook and stir over medium heat until boiling. Remove from heat. Chill until syrupy.

In medium size bowl combine raspberry gelatin with boiling water. Stir to dissolve. Mix in cranberry sauce, celery and nuts. Chill until thickening stage.

Whip cream until stiff and fold into thickened pudding and jelly mixture. Fold in nutmeg. Pour into mold. Chill until a bit firm then pour thickened cranberry mixture over top. Chill overnight. Unmolded on frilly looking lettuce, this highlights any table.

Paré Pointer

God gives every bird its food, but does not throw it into the nest.

Such a pretty salad. A shimmering delight.

Peach-flavored gelatin	1 – 3 oz.	1 – 85 g
Boiling water	1 cup	225 mL
Peach juice (add water if needed)	1 cup	225 mL
Almond flavoring	¼ tsp.	1 mL
Whipping cream		
(or 1 envelope topping)	1 cup	250 mL
Sliced peaches, drained	14 oz.	398 mL

Dissolve gelatin in boiling water in medium size bowl.

Add juice and flavoring. Stir. Measure out 1 cup (225 mL) jelly into medium size bowl and chill until syrupy. Leave remainder of jelly at room temperature.

Whip cream until stiff. Fold into the thickened jelly. Pour into mold. Chill. Put remainder of jelly in refrigerator to chill until syrupy.

Fold peaches into thickened clear jelly. Spoon over first layer. Chill until firm. Serves 6.

Pictured on page 89.

Pare Pointer

If you stand for nothing, you will fall for something.

CUCUMBER SPECIAL EVENT

Creamy good. Perks up any table. A favorite.

Lime-flavored gelatin	1 – 3 oz.	1 – 85 g
Boiling water	¾ cup	150 mL
Salad dressing	1 cup	225 mL
Cream cheese, slivered in	4 oz.	125 g
Horseradish	1 tsp.	5 mL
Lemon juice	2 tbsp.	30 mL
Unpeeled cucumber, seeded and grated	¾ cup	150 mL
Finely chopped onion	¼ cup	50 mL

Dissolve gelatin in boiling water. Let stand for 5-10 minutes to cool slightly.

Add salad dressing and whisk or beat in. Sliver in cream cheese. Add horseradish and lemon juice. Chill until syrupy.

Cut cucumber in half lengthwise. Remove seeds. Grate, then squeeze to get juice out. Fold into thickened jelly along with onion. Pour into mold or serving bowl. Chill.

COLLEEN VEGETABLE MOLD

An old stand-by. It is still as good as ever.

Lime-flavored gelatin	1 – 3 oz.	1 – 85 g
Boiling water	1 cup	225 mL
Crushed pineapple with juice	1 cup	225 mL
Salt	¼ tsp.	1 mL
Granulated sugar	2 tsp.	10 mL
Salad dressing	¼ cup	50 mL
Cottage cheese	1 cup	250 mL
Chopped celery	½ cup	125 mL
Shredded carrot	½ cup	125 mL

Dissolve gelatin in boiling water. Add pineapple, salt and sugar. Stir. Chill until syrupy stirring once or twice.

Fold salad dressing into thickened jelly. Add cottage cheese, celery and carrot. Fold in. Pour into mold or bowl. Chill.

PERFECT CUCUMBER SALAD

Sparkling clear, excellent choice, but try the variations as well.

Lime-flavored gelatin	1 – 3 oz.	1 – 85 g
Boiling water	½ cup	125 mL
Lemon juice	2 tbsp.	30 mL
Salt	¼ tsp.	1 mL
Grated onion (or 1 tbsp., 15 mL, onion flakes)	¼ cup	50 mL
Grated cucumber, with skin on	1 cup	250 mL

Dissolve gelatin in boiling water. Stir in lemon juice, salt and onion. Use the fine size of the three common graters to grate the cucumber. Do not drain. Add to jelly. Chill until slightly thickened, stirring occasionally. Pour into mold. Chill.

CUCUMBER SOUR CREAM SALAD: Add 1 cup (250 mL) sour cream to thickened jelly. Pour into mold. Chill. It is like a completely different salad, creamy and soft.

LAYERED CUCUMBER SALAD: Spoon half of thickened jelly mixture in bottom of mold. Chill. When almost firm, stir ½ cup (125 mL) sour cream into second half of thickened jelly. Spoon over top of first layer in mold. Chill.

CUCUMBER SALAD

What a fancy way to eat cucumbers!

Lime-flavored gelatin	1 – 3 oz.	1 – 85 g
Salt	½ tsp.	2 mL
Boiling water	1 cup	225 mL
Crushed pineapple and juice	14 oz.	398 mL
Dry onion flakes	1 tsp.	5 mL
Salad dressing	½ cup	125 mL
Cucumber, chopped and drained	1 cup	250 mL

In medium size bowl combine gelatin, salt and boiling water. Stir to dissolve. Add crushed pineapple and onion, Stir. Chill until syrupy, stirring once or twice.

Fold in salad dressing until blended. Fold in cucumber. Pour into mold. Chill.

COLLEEN SALAD

A pretty creamy green color. Quick to prepare. Uses up that cottage cheese that is left.

Lime-flavored gelatin	1 – 3 oz.	1 – 85 g
Boiling water	1 cup	225 mL
Salt	¼ tsp.	1 mL
Crushed pineapple with juice	1 cup	225 mL
Cottage cheese	1 cup	250 mL

Mix gelatin, water and salt together. Stir to dissolve. Stir in pineapple with juice. Chill until syrupy.

Fold cottage cheese into thickened mixture. Pour into mold or bowl. Chill.

COLLEEN VEGETABLE SALAD: Add ¼ cup (50 mL) salad dressing, ½ cup (125 mL) chopped celery and ½ cup (125 mL) grated carrot. An old standby.

ORANGE COLLEEN SALAD: Use orange gelatin in place of lime. Add ¼ tsp. (1 mL) powdered ginger.

LIME CHEESE MOLD: Use 14 oz. (398 mL) crushed pineapple and juice. Omit cottage cheese. Add 4 oz. (125 g) cream cheese slivered in and ⅓ cup (75 mL) chopped nuts.

1. Orange Onion Salad page 34
2. Spring Salad page 46
3. Fruit Platter page 43
   (a) Kiwi Fruit
   (b) Cantaloupe Balls
   (c) Honeydew Balls
   (d) Strawberries
4. Condensed Milk Dressing page 145

SEVEN UP SALAD

A cool lime colored melt-in-your-mouth goodness.

Seven Up soft drink (or other)	1 cup	250 mL
Small marshmallows	2 cups	500 mL
Lime-flavored gelatin	1 – 3 oz.	1 – 85 g
Cream cheese, cut up	8 oz.	250 g
Crushed pineapple with juice	14 oz.	398 mL
Whipping cream (or 1 envelope topping)	1 cup	250 mL
Salad dressing	½ cup	125 mL

Put Seven Up and marshmallows into medium saucepan. Heat and stir over medium heat to melt marshmallows.

Stir in gelatin to dissolve. Add cream cheese. Stir until melted. Remove from heat. Stir in pineapple. Chill until syrupy.

Whip cream until stiff. Add salad dressing. Fold into thickened jelly. Pour into mold or pretty serving bowl. Chill. Serves 10 to 12.

LIME CRUNCH SALAD

Creamy mint green color, this is chunky and crunchy. Delicious.

Lime-flavored gelatin	1 – 3 oz.	1 – 85 g
Boiling water	1 cup	225 mL
Salad dressing	1 cup	225 mL
Cottage cheese	1 cup	250 mL
Diced cucumber, drained	½ cup	125 mL
Diced celery	½ cup	125 mL
Chopped walnuts or pecans	½ cup	125 mL
Dry onion flakes	1 tbsp.	15 mL

Combine gelatin and boiling water in bowl. Stir to dissolve. Whisk or beat in salad dressing. Chill until syrupy.

Fold in cottage cheese, drained cucumber, celery, nuts and onion. Pour into mold or bowl. Chill.

CABBAGE PIMENTO SALAD

Definitely the leader in its class. Party perfect.

Lime-flavored gelatin	1 – 3 oz.	1 – 85 g
Boiling water	1 cup	225 mL
Small marshmallows	1 cup	250 mL
Shredded cabbage	2 cups	500 mL
Chopped pimento	¼ cup	50 mL
Crushed pineapple with juice	14 oz.	398 mL
Mayonnaise	1 cup	225 mL
Whipping cream		
(or 1 envelope topping)	1 cup	250 mL
Walnuts, finely chopped	1 cup	250 mL

Combine gelatin and boiling water in bowl. Stir to dissolve. Add marshmallows. Stir until melted.

Add cabbage, pimento, pineapple with juice and mayonnaise. Chill until it begins to thicken. Stir once or twice.

Whip cream until stiff. Fold into thickened cabbage mixture. Fold in nuts. Turn into 3 quart (3 L) mold. Chill.

LIME VEGETABLE MOLD

Makes a clear vegetable packed salad.

Lime-flavored gelatin	1 – 3 oz.	1 – 85 g
Boiling water	¾ cup	175 mL
Salt	¼ tsp.	1 mL
Cold water	¾ cup	175 mL
Shredded cabbage	1 cup	250 mL
Grated carrot	½ cup	125 mL
Diced celery	½ cup	125 mL

Dissolve gelatin in boiling water in bowl. Stir in salt. Add cold water. Chill until slightly thickened.

Add cabbage, carrot and celery to thickened jelly. Fold in. Pour into mold. Chill. Garnish with sliced cucumbers or other vegetable.

Pictured on page 89.

FLUFFY VEGETABLE MEDLEY

A good, fluffy mint green-color salad — a disguise for vegetables.

Lime-flavored gelatin	1 – 3 oz.	1 – 85 g
Boiling water	1 cup	250 mL
Salt	¼ tsp.	1 mL
Granulated sugar	1 tbsp.	15 mL
Cold water	½ cup	75 mL
Salad dressing	½ cup	125 mL
Grated cabbage	2 cups	500 mL
Grated carrot	½ cup	125 mL
Chopped celery	½ cup	125 mL
Chopped cucumber	¼ cup	50 mL
Grated onion (or 1 tsp. (5 mL) onion flakes)	1 tbsp.	15 mL

Dissolve gelatin in boiling water in bowl. Stir in salt and sugar. Add cold water. Whisk or beat in salad dressing to combine. Chill until slightly thickened. Beat with rotary beater until fluffy.

Fold in cabbage, carrot, celery, cucumber and onion. Pour into mold or serving bowl. Chill.

Note: Jelly may be completely set then put in a blender to fluff before adding vegetables. It will make it nice and airy but it won't increase the volume as much.

PINEAPPLE SOUR CREAM SALAD

Creamy green, somewhat tart and so easy.

Lime-flavored gelatin	1 – 3 oz.	1 – 85 g
Boiling water	1 cup	225 mL
Crushed pineapple and juice	14 oz.	398 mL
Sour cream	1 cup	250 mL

Put gelatin in bowl. Stir in boiling water to dissolve. Add pineapple. Stir. Chill until syrupy.

Stir sour cream into thickened jelly. Pour into mold or serving bowl. Chill.

LIME PEAR SALAD

Wonderful for a luncheon. Creamy and light.

Lime-flavored gelatin	1 – 3 oz.	1 – 85 g
Boiling water	1 cup	225 mL
Pear juice	1 cup	225 mL
Cream cheese	4 oz.	125 g
Small marshmallows	100	100
(or 12 large, cut up)		
Canned pear halves, diced	8	8
Whipping cream		
(or 1 envelope topping)	1 cup	250 mL

In a large bowl put gelatin and boiling water. Stir to dissolve.

Add pear juice. Using wire cheese cutter, cut cheese in small chunks. Stir in marshmallows. Chill, stirring now and then until mixture begins to thicken.

Fold in diced pears. Whip cream until stiff. Fold into mixture. Pour into mold or serving bowl. For long standing in a warm room, better to use a serving bowl since this is not too firm a salad. Serves 12.

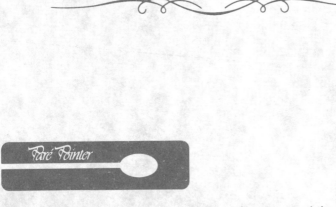

Pare Pointer

Shouldn't there be a course taught on how to read the handwriting on the wall?

One of the best cranberry salads. Delicious tasting.

Envelope unflavored gelatin	¼ oz.	7 g
Cold water	¼ cup	50 mL
Strawberry-flavored gelatin	1 – 3 oz.	1 – 85 g
Boiling water	1 cup	225 mL
Medium size orange	1	1
Grated rind from second orange	1	1
Whole cranberry sauce	14 oz.	398 mL

Sprinkle unflavored gelatin over cold water. Let stand for 5 minutes.

Dissolve strawberry gelatin in boiling water. Add softened gelatin. Stir to dissolve. Grate orange and add rind to jelly. Cut off pith (white part) and cut up orange into small pieces. Add to jelly. Grate second orange and add peel only to jelly. Stir in cranberry sauce. Chill until syrupy. Stir and chill.

Note: Cherry or raspberry gelatin may be used rather than strawberry.

Pictured on page 89.

A frothy goodness. An excellent frosty pink luncheon choice. Delicious.

Stawberry-flavored gelatin	2 – 3oz.	2 – 85 g
Boiling water	1 cup	225 mL
Crushed pineapple and juice	1 cup	225 mL
Frozen strawberries, thawed	½ of 15 oz.	½ of 425 g
Small marshmallows	3 cups	750 mL
Whipping cream		
(or 1 envelope topping)	1 cup	250 mL
Chopped nuts	¼ cup	50 mL

Combine gelatin with boiling water. Stir to dissolve. Add pineapple and strawberries. Chill to the syrup stage.

Add marshmallows. Whip cream until stiff. Fold into jelly along with nuts. Pour into mold or 9 × 9 inch (22 × 22 cm) pan.

STRAWBERRY MOLD

A delicious delicate flavor. Strawberry red color.

Strawberry-flavored gelatin	2 – 3 oz.	2 – 85 g
Boiling water	1 cup	225 mL
Crushed pineapple with juice	14 oz.	398 mL
Frozen strawberries, thawed	15 oz.	425 g

Put gelatin in medium bowl. Add boiling water. Stir to dissolve.

Mix in pineapple and strawberries. Chill until syrupy. Stir and pour into mold or bowl. Chill.

STRAWBERRY BANANA

A good combination of flavors.

Strawberry-flavored gelatin	2 – 3 oz.	2 – 85 g
Boiling water	2 cups	450 mL
Frozen strawberries, thawed	15 oz.	425 g
Crushed pineapple and juice	14 oz.	398 mL
Mashed bananas	3	3

Put gelatin and boiling water in bowl. Stir to dissolve.

Add strawberries, pineapple and bananas. Chill until syrupy. Stir. Pour into mold or bowl. Chill.

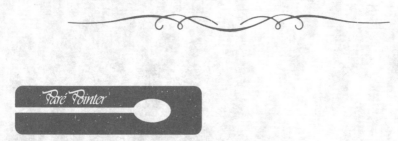

At least you aren't alone when you are frustrated because you are beside yourself.

BING CHERRY SALAD

A luncheon favorite. Creamy pink with dark cherries. A delicious nutty taste.

Cherry-flavored gelatin	2 – 3 oz.	2 – 85 g
Cherry juice and water	1½ cups	325 mL
Crushed pineapple and juice	14 oz.	398 mL
Bing cherries, drained, pitted and halved	14 oz.	398 mL
Sour cream	1 cup	225 mL
Chopped walnuts	½ cup	125 mL

Put gelatin in saucepan with cherry juice and water. Heat and stir over medium heat to dissolve. Remove from heat. Stir in crushed pineapple. Chill until syrupy.

Add halved and pitted cherries, sour cream and walnuts. Stir. Pour into mold and chill. Unmold on lettuce. If using square pan, place each salad section on top of lettuce on pretty plate.

BLUEBERRY SALAD

A luscious portion would be welcomed by young and old.

Grape–flavored gelatin	2 – 3 oz.	2 – 85 g
Boiling water	2 cups	450 mL
Crushed pineapple with juice	14 oz.	398 mL
Blueberry pie filling	19 oz.	540 mL
Cream cheese, softened	8 oz.	250 g
Sour cream	1 cup	250 mL
Granulated sugar	½ cup	125 mL
Vanilla	1 tbsp.	15 mL
Chopped pecans or walnuts for sprinkling.		

Pour gelatin and water into bowl. Stir to dissolve. Stir in pineapple and pie filling. Pour into 9 × 9 inch (22 × 22 cm) pan. Chill until firm.

Combine cream cheese, sour cream, sugar and vanilla in mixing bowl. Beat until blended. Spread over chilled, firm jelly.

Sprinkle nuts over top. Serves 9-12.

PINK VELVET

Three ingredients and three minutes to make this salad. Smooooth!

Strawberry–flavored gelatin	1 – 3 oz.	1 – 85 g
Boiling water	1 cup	225 mL
Sour cream	1 cup	250 mL

Dissolve gelatin in boiling water in small bowl. Beat in sour cream. A whisk works well. Pour into mold or bowl. Chill.

BING COLA SALAD

Dark and shimmering! The cola drink is the secret to the flavor.

Cherry-flavored gelatin	2 – 3 oz.	2 – 85 g
Cherry juice and water to make	2 cups	425 mL
Cola soft drink	1½ cups	375 mL
Bing cherries well drained, halved and pitted	14 oz.	398 mL
Chopped walnuts	½ cup	125 mL

Put gelatin, cherry juice and water in small saucepan. Heat and stir over medium heat until dissolved. Remove from heat. Stir in cola drink, cherries and nuts. Chill until syrupy. Stir. Pour into mold or bowl. Chill.

STRAWBERRY CREAM CHEESE

Not many ingredients in this one. Gorgeous shade of red.

Strawberry-flavored gelatin	2 – 3 oz.	2 – 85 g
Boiling water	2 cups	450 mL
Cream cheese	4 oz.	250 g
Frozen strawberries, thawed	½ of 15 oz.	½ of 425 g

Put gelatin and boiling water into bowl. Stir to dissolve. Cut in cream cheese — the smaller the pieces, the nicer it will look. Add berries and juice. Chill until syrupy. Stir to distribute cheese evenly. Pour into mold or bowl. Chill.

RASPBERRY CREAM

Blushing pink with excellent flavor and eye appeal.

Raspberry-flavored gelatin	1 – 3 oz.	1 – 85 g
Boiling water	¾ cup	175 mL
Granulated sugar	¼ cup	50 mL
Package frozen		
raspberries, thawed	15 oz.	425 g
Whipping cream		
(or 1 envelope topping)	1 cup	250 mL
Small marshmallows	1 cup	250 mL

Dissolve gelatin in boiling water in medium bowl. Add sugar. Stir to dissolve. Stir in raspberries. Chill until syrupy stirring once or twice.

Whip cream until stiff. Fold into thickened jelly. Fold in marshmallows. Pour into mold or bowl. Chill.

RASPBERRY NUT SALAD

Raspberry red, a glossy mold.

Raspberry-flavored gelatin	1 – 3 oz.	1 – 85 g
Boiling water	1 cup	250 mL
Raspberry juice (plus		
water if needed)	¾ cup	150 mL
Frozen raspberries, thawed		
and drained	½ of 15 oz.	½ of 425 g
Diced banana	1	1
Sliced brazil nuts	½ cup	125 mL

Dissolve gelatin in boiling water in bowl. Stir in raspberry juice. Chill until syrupy.

Stir in drained raspberries, banana and nuts. Pour into mold or bowl. Chill.

RASPBERRY MALLOW SALAD

Both taste and color appeal here. Very showy.

Raspberry-flavored gelatin	6 oz.	170 g
Boiling water	1 cup	225 mL
Frozen raspberries, thawed	15 oz.	425 g
Applesauce	14 oz.	398 mL
Small marshmallows	2 cups	500 mL
Sour cream	2 cups	500 mL

Dissolve gelatin in boiling water in saucepan. Heat and stir to dissolve. Remove from heat.

Stir in raspberries and apple sauce. Pour into 9 × 9 inch (22 × 22 cm) pan. Chill until firm.

Put marshmallows and sour cream in blender. Do not blend but allow to stand for 2 hours. Then blend until smooth. Spread over firm jelly. Serves 9-12.

STRAWBERRY COCKTAIL

Serve for an after meeting lunch with rolls or baking powder biscuits. Creamy pink.

Strawberry-flavored gelatin	1 – 3 oz.	1 – 85 g
Boiling water	1 cup	225 mL
Small marshmallows	1 cup	250 mL
Frozen strawberries, thawed	½ of 15 oz.	½ of 425 g
Fruit cocktail, drained	14 oz.	398 mL
Whipping cream (or 1 envelope topping)	1 cup	250 mL

Dissolve gelatin in boiling water. Add marshmallows. Stir until melted.

Add strawberries and drained fruit cocktail. Chill until consistency of syrup.

Whip cream until stiff. Fold into thickened jelly. Pour into mold, bowl or 8 × 8 inch (20 × 20 cm) pan. Serve on lettuce, shredded or leaf.

Serve with baking powder biscuits or small rolls for a terrific get-together snack.

Lemon-flavored gelatin	1 – 3 oz.	1 – 85 g
Boiling water	1 cup	225 mL
Cold water	½ cup	125 mL
Mayonnaise	¼ cup	50 mL
Diced red apple, unpeeled	1 cup	250 mL
Colored tiny marshmallows	1 cup	250 mL
Diced banana	½ cup	125 mL
Diced green grapes	1 cup	250 mL
Whipping cream		
(or 1 envelope topping)	1 cup	250 mL

Lettuce

Dissolve gelatin in boiling water in medium size bowl. Stir in cold water. Chill until it begins to thicken.

Add mayonnaise, apple, marshmallows, banana and grapes to slightly thickened jelly.

Whip cream until stiff. Fold into jelly. Turn into 9 x 9 inch (22 x 22 cm) pan. Chill overnight. Serve on shredded or whole leaf lettuce. Spoon fruit dressing over top. Serves 9-12.

FRUIT DRESSING

Juice of lemon	1	1
Pineapple juice	¾ cup	175 mL
Cornstarch	1 tbsp.	15 mL
Salt	⅛ tsp.	½ mL
Egg yolk	1	1
Granulated sugar	¼ cup	50 mL
Egg White	1	1
Whipping cream	¼ cup	50 mL

Put lemon and pineapple juice in top of double boiler. Add cornstarch and salt. Stir well. Cook until thickened over boiling water.

In small bowl, combine egg yolk with sugar. Stir into hot mixture until thickened, about 3 minutes. Remove from heat.

Beat egg white until stiff. Carefully fold into hot mixture. Cool.

Whip cream until stiff. Fold into cooled dressing before serving.

EGG SOUFFLE

Wonderful hot weather food. Fluffy and good.

Lemon-flavored gelatin	1 – 3 oz.	1 – 85 g
Boiling water	1 cup	225 mL
Cold water	½ cup	100 mL
Mayonnaise	½ cup	125 mL
Vinegar	1 tbsp.	15 mL
Salt	½ tsp.	2 mL
Pepper	⅛ tsp.	½ mL
Hard boiled eggs, chopped fine	3	3
Chopped celery (fine)	½ cup	125 mL
Diced green pepper	1 tbsp.	15 mL
Diced pimento	1 tbsp.	15 mL
Minced onion	1 tbsp.	15 mL

Dissolve gelatin in boiling water.

Add cold water, mayonnaise, vinegar, salt and pepper. Whisk or beat together. Chill until quite syrupy. Beat until fluffy.

Add eggs, celery, green pepper, pimento and onion. Pour into mold or glass bowl. Chill.

BEET MOLD

Pretty with or without the apple. Snap it up with more horseradish if you prefer.

Lemon-flavored gelatin	1 – 3 oz.	1 – 85 g
Boiling water	1½ cups	350 mL
Lemon juice or cider vinegar	1 tbsp.	15 mL
Horseradish	2-3 tsp.	10-15 mL
Dry onion flakes	1 tsp.	5 mL
Apple, peeled and diced (optional)	1	1
Beets, drained and diced	14 oz.	398 mL

Dissolve gelatin in boiling water. Stir in lemon juice, horseradish and onion flakes. Chill until syrupy.

Add apple and beets to thickened jelly. Mix and pour into mold or serving bowl. Chill.

TOMATO ASPIC

The easy way to make a good familiar salad.

Lemon-flavored gelatin	1 – 3 oz.	1 – 85 g
Tomato juice	1⅔ cups	375 mL
Salt	½ tsp.	2 mL
Pinch of pepper		
Onion powder	¼ tsp.	2 mL
Apple, peeled and chopped fine	½ cup	100 mL
Celery, chopped fine	¼ cup	50 mL

Put gelatin, tomato juice, salt, pepper and onion powder in medium size saucepan. Heat and stir over medium heat until jelly crystals are dissolved. Chill until syrupy. Stir now and then.

Fold apple and celery into thickening jelly. Pour into mold or a serving dish.

Pictured on page 89.

Variation: Apple may be omitted and amount of celery increased. Apple and celery may both be omitted for a tasty, smooth salad.

TOMATO SHRIMP ASPIC: Add 1 tin of rinsed and drained shrimp to thickened jelly.

COTTAGE CHEESE MOLD

A mild flavored, creamy yellow salad with pretty red bits showing here and there. A good way to dress up cottage cheese.

Lemon-flavored gelatin	1 – 3 oz.	1 – 85 g
Boiling water	1 cup	225 mL
Crushed pineapple and juice	14 oz.	398 mL
Cottage cheese	1 cup	250 mL
Chopped walnuts	⅓ cup	75 mL
Maraschino cherries, quartered	¼ cup	50 mL
Whipping cream (or envelope topping)	1 cup	250 mL

Dissolve gelatin in boiling water in medium bowl. Stir in pineapple. Chill until syrupy.

Add cottage cheese, nuts and cherries to thickened jelly. Whip cream until stiff. Fold into jelly. Pour into mold or bowl. Chill.

PIMENTO SALAD

Compliments meat dishes — especially barbeques. A pretty yellow with red and green bits showing throughout.

Lemon-flavored gelatin	3 oz.	85 g
Boiling water	1 cup	225 mL
Crushed pineapple and juice	14 oz.	398 mL
Cream cheese	4 oz.	125 g
Chopped pimento (small container)	¼ cup	50 mL
Celery, chopped fine	½ cup	125 mL
Chopped nuts	½ cup	125 mL
Whipping cream (or 1 envelope topping)	1 cup	250 mL

Dissolve gelatin in boiling water in small bowl. Stir in pineapple.

Have cheese at room temperature. Mix cream cheese with chopped pimentos. A fork works well, stirring and mashing a bit. Stir into jelly.

Add celery and nuts. Chill until syrupy.

Whip cream until stiff. Fold into thickened jelly. Pour into mold or bowl. Chill.

FISH GARNISH

Just the tartness needed to compliment any fish. And it is excellent with meat too.

Lemon-flavored gelatin	2 – 3 oz.	2 – 85 g
Boiling water	2 cups	450 mL
Vinegar	½ cup	125 mL
Mayonnaise	1 tbsp.	15 mL
Sweet pickle relish	1 cup	225 mL
Chopped green pepper	⅔ cup	150 mL
Grated onion	¼ cup	50 mL

Dissolve gelatin in boiling water. Stir in vinegar. Chill until syrupy.

Whisk or beat in mayonnaise.

Fold relish, green pepper and onion into thickened jelly. Pour into mold or serving bowl. Chill several hours. Serves 6-8.

LEMON CHEDDAR SALAD

This must be the quickest of the special salads. Showy and extremely good. A party special.

Lemon-flavored gelatin	1 – 3 oz.	1 – 85 g
Boiling water	1 cup	225 mL
Crushed pineapple and juice	14 oz.	398 mL
Whipping cream		
(or 1 envelope topping)	1 cup	250 mL
Grated cheddar cheese	1 cup	250 mL

Combine gelatin and boiling water in bowl. Stir to dissolve.

Stir in crushed pineapple and juice. Chill until of egg white consistency.

Whip cream until stiff. Fold into thickened jelly. Fold in grated cheese. Pour into your prettiest bowl. Chill. Garnish with orange slices if desired. Serves 10.

Pictured on cover.

MARSHMALLOW CHEDDAR: Add 1 cup (250 mL) small marshmallows with whipped cream and grated cheese.

MINCEMEAT SALAD

Serve this different and spicy salad with your meat dishes.

Lemon-flavored gelatin	1 – 3 oz.	1 – 85 g
Orange juice	1 cup	250 mL
Mincemeat (puréed)	¾ cup	150 mL
Apple sauce	¼ cup	50 mL
Finely chopped walnuts	¼ cup	50 mL

Put gelatin and orange juice into small saucepan. Heat and stir until dissolved.

Purée mincemeat in blender. It isn't necessary but breaks suet down. Pour into jelly. Stir in apple sauce and nuts. Pour into mold or bowl. Chill, stirring once or twice. Serves 6.

ROYAL CRANBERRY RASPBERRY RING

A shimmering beauty! Great flavor. Great compliments when you serve it.

Lemon-flavored gelatin	1 – 3 oz.	1 – 85 g
Unflavored gelatin powder	1–¼ oz.	1–7 g
Boiling water	1½ cups	375 mL
Package of frozen raspberries	10 oz.	284 g
Whole cranberry sauce	1 cup	250 mL
Grated rind of orange	1	1
Lemon lime soft drink	1 cup	225 mL

In medium size bowl put both gelatin powders. Stir together to mix thoroughly. Add boiling water stirring to dissolve. Add frozen raspberries. Use a fork to break up pieces. Stir to mix well.

Stir in cranberry sauce and orange rind. Chill until consistency of egg white.

Gently fold in lemon lime soft drink using folding (up and over) motion. Chill until it begins to thicken. Pour into 4-4½ cup (1L) ring mold. Chill several hours.

Variation: Omit whole cranberry sauce and grated orange rind. Add one cup (250 mL) cranberry orange relish.

1. Tomato Aspic page 85
2. Dill Pickle Salad page 94
3. Peaches And Cream page 67
4. Lime Vegetable Mold page 74
5. Cranberry Mold page 77

PINEAPPLE ORANGE SALAD

Makes a pretty combination.

Lemon-flavored gelatin	2–3 oz.	2–85 g
Boiling water	2 cups	450 mL
Crushed pineapple and juice	14 oz.	398 mL
Mandarin orange segments, drained	12 oz.	341 mL
Cottage cheese	2 cups	500 mL
Whipping cream		
(or 2 envelopes topping)	2 cups	500 mL

Dissolve gelatin in boiling water in medium bowl. Stir in pineapple. Chill until syrupy.

Add orange sections and cottage cheese. Whip cream until stiff. Fold into thickened jelly. Pour into mold or bowl. Chill.

JELLIED FRUIT SALAD

This is one of the prettiest fruit salads. Makes a gorgeous mold.

Lemon-flavored gelatin	2 – 3 oz.	2 – 85 g
Ginger ale	2 cups	450 mL
Frozen strawberries, almost thawed	10 oz.	184 g
Grapefruit sections, drained	14 oz.	398 mL
Pineapple chunks, drained	14 oz.	398 mL

Combine gelatin with ginger ale in small saucepan. Heat and stir over medium heat until dissolved. Stir in strawberries, grapefruit and pineapple. You may prefer to cut grapefruit sections in half. Chill until syrupy, then pour into mold or use 8 × 8 inch (20 × 20 cm) pan and serve with Fruit Sauce Topping, page 140.

Pare Pointer

Anger opens the mouth and shuts the mind.

PINEAPPLE CREAM SALAD

Rich and creamy — everybody's favorite. My favorite.

Lemon-flavored gelatin	1 – 3 oz.	1 – 85 g
Boiling water	1 cup	225 mL
Crushed pineapple and juice	14 oz.	398 mL
Cream cheese	4 oz.	125 g
Small marshmallows	100	100
Whipping cream		
(or 1 envelope topping)	1 cup	250 mL

Combine gelatin with boiling water in fairly large bowl. Stir to dissolve.

Add pineapple with juice. Using wire cheese cutter, cut in cheese. Add marshmallows. Stir. Chill until it begins to thicken, stirring occasionally.

Whip cream until stiff. Fold into thickened mixture. Pour into a pretty serving bowl. Chill. This salad doesn't hold very well since it isn't too firm but will stand for a short time if molded. Serves 12.

ASPARAGUS MOLD

Not an ordinary salad. Mild flavored. Fresh cooked asparagus gives a nice color.

Lemon-flavored gelatin	1 – 3 oz.	1 – 85 g
Boiling water	1 cup	225 mL
Cold water	¾ cup	150 mL
Dry onion flakes	1 tsp.	5 mL
Salt	¼ tsp.	2 mL
Cut asparagus, drained (or fresh)	10 oz.	284 mL
Chopped celery	½ cup	125 mL
Chopped pimento	2 tbsp.	30 mL

Put gelatin and boiling water in bowl. Stir to dissolve. Stir in cold water, onion and salt. Chill until syrupy.

Fold asparagus, celery and pimento into thickened jelly. Pour into mold or bowl. Chill.

ASPARAGUS CHEESE MOLD: Add ½ cup (125 mL) grated cheese to salad. Omit pimento or include it. It is optional.

This is the way to make Waldorf the day before. Light and fluffy.

Lemon-flavored gelatin	1 – 3 oz.	1 – 85 g
Boiling water	1 cup	250 mL
Cold water	½ cup	125 mL
Lemon juice	1 tbsp.	15 mL
Salt	¼ tsp.	2 mL
Eating apple, unpeeled and diced	1	1
Diced celery	1 cup	250 mL
Chopped walnuts	¼ cup	50 mL
Mayonnaise or salad dressing	¼ cup	50 mL
Whipping cream (or 1 envelope topping)	1 cup	250 mL

Dissolve gelatin in boiling water. Stir in cold water, lemon juice and salt. Chill until syrupy.

Fold apple, celery, nuts and mayonnaise into jelly.

Beat cream until stiff. Fold into jelly. Pour into mold or serving bowl. Chill. Serves 8-10.

Variation: Add ¼ cup (50 mL) raisins.

CRANBERRY LEMON SALAD

Rather than a cranberry color throughout, this is a mottled mold.

Lemon-flavored gelatin	1 – 3 oz.	1 – 85 g
Boiling water	1 cup	225 mL
Crushed pineapple with juice	14 oz.	398 mL
Celery, chopped fine	½ cup	125 mL
Whole cranberry sauce	1 cup	250 mL

Combine gelatin with water in bowl stirring to dissolve. Add pineapple. Chill until syrupy.

Fold celery and cranberry sauce into thickened jelly. Pour into mold or bowl. Chill.

DILL PICKLE SALAD

A very pretty lemon-lime color dotted with red bits. Great with baked fish. Good with meat and ham too.

Lemon-flavored gelatin	1 – 3 oz.	1 – 85 g
Boiling water	1 cup	250 mL
Crushed pineapple and juice	14 oz.	398 mL
Lemon juice	2 tbsp.	30 mL
Dill pickles, chopped fine	½ cup	125 mL
Chopped pimento	2 tbsp.	30 mL

Combine gelatin with water in medium bowl. Stir to dissolve. Add pineapple, lemon juice, dill and pimento. Chill until syrupy. Stir to distribute evenly throughout. Pour into mold or bowl. Chill.

Pictured on page 89.

TOMATO CHEESE MOLD

Very good with any meat.

Lemon-flavored gelatin	3 oz.	85 g
Cream of tomato soup	10 oz.	284 mL
Mayonnaise	1 cup	250 mL
Cream cheese	8 oz.	250 g
Chopped celery	1 cup	250 mL
Finely chopped green pepper	½ cup	125 mL
Dried onion flakes	1 tbsp.	15 mL
Blanched sliced almonds	¼ cup	50 mL
Red food coloring (optional)		

In small saucepan put gelatin and soup. Heat and stir over medium heat until dissolved. Cool.

In small mixing bowl, beat mayonnaise and cream cheese together well. Stir in celery, green pepper, onion and almonds. Add food coloring to perk up color if desired. Add jelly mixture. Stir. Pour into mold or bowl. Chill, stirring once or twice. Serves 8-10.

QUICK APPLESAUCE SALAD

As refreshing as a cool summer drink.

Lemon or lime-flavored gelatin	1 – 3 oz.	1 – 85 g
Seven Up soft drink	1 cup	250 mL
Apple sauce	1 cup	200 mL

Combine gelatin and Seven Up in small saucepan. Heat and stir until dissolve. Remove from heat. Stir in applesauce. Pour into bowl or mold. Chill. Serves 4.

LAYERED APPLE SALAD: Put one half into mold. Chill until firm. Whip ½ cup (125 mL) cream until stiff. Fold into second half of thickened jelly. Spoon over first half. Chill. Serves 4-6.

GOLDEN GLOW

A simple salad, pretty and popular. Makes a glistening mold. Try using a strawberry-flavored gelatin sometime.

Lemon-flavored gelatin	1–3 oz.	1–85 g
Boiling Water	1 cup	225 mL
Salt	¼ tsp.	1 mL
Crushed pineapple with juice	1 cup	225 mL
Grated carrot	½ cup	125 mL
Celery, finely chopped	¼ cup	50 mL

Combine gelatin, boiling water and salt. Stir to dissolve. Stir in pineapple and juice. Chill until starting to thicken.

Fold in carrot and celery. Pour into mold. Chill.

CREAMY LEMON SALAD: Fold 1 cup (250 mL) cream whipped (or 1 envelope topping) into thickened salad. Makes quite a different creamy salad.

CREAMY LIME SALAD: Use lime gelatin instead of lemon. Fold 1 cup (250 mL) cream whipped (or 1 envelope topping) into thickened salad. Different color but similar taste as Creamy Lemon.

CREAMY ORANGE SALAD: Use orange gelatin instead of lemon. Fold 1 cup (250 mL) cream whipped (or 1 envelope topping) into thickened salad. Gives a color variation while keeping a similar flavor.

GOLD SLAW: Omit celery. Add 1 cup (250 mL) shredded cabbage.

Note: True Golden Glow contains no celery. Omit it if you like. Try it with orange gelatin for a superb flavor.

MOLDED CRANBERRY SALAD

Made from raw cranberries, this is very good.

Orange-flavored gelatin	1 – 3 oz.	1 – 85 g
Unflavored gelatin	1 – ¼ oz.	1 – 7 g
Boiling water	1 cup	250 mL
Lemon juice	3 tbsp.	50 mL
Granulated sugar	1 cup	250 mL
Ground cranberries, fresh or frozen	2 cups	500 mL
Finely chopped celery	1 cup	250 mL
Chopped walnuts	½ cup	125 mL

Put gelatin powders into bowl. Stir to mix completely. Add boiling water. Stir to dissolve. Add lemon juice and sugar. Stir to dissolve sugar. Cool until syrupy.

Add cranberries to thickened jelly. Stir in celery and nuts. Pour into ring mold or bowl. Chill.

APRICOT SALAD

Flavors blend well in this quick salad.

Orange-flavored gelatin	1 – 3 oz.	1 – 85 g
Hot water	1 cup	225 mL
Apricots, drained and cut	2 – 14 oz.	2 – 398 mL
Crushed pineapple with juice	14 oz.	398 mL
Mayonnaise for garnish		

Dissolve gelatin in hot water.

Add drained apricots cut in half or in quarters depending on size. Stir in pineapple. Chill stirring once or twice until syrupy.

Pour thickened jelly into mold or serving bowl. Chill. Top with a dollop of mayonnaise before serving. Serves 6-8.

APRICOT PINEAPPLE SALAD

Don't know what to serve for your after-meeting-lunch?

Orange-flavored gelatin	2 – 3 oz.	2 – 85 g
Boiling water	2 cups	450 mL
Apricot, pineapple and orange juice (measure 2 cups (450 mL), set aside ½ cup (125 mL) for dressing)	1½ cups	325 mL
Apricots, drained and cut up	14 oz.	398 mL
Crushed pineapple, drained	14 oz.	398 mL
Small marshmallows	1 cup	250 mL

Dissolve gelatin in boiling water in bowl. Stir in apricot, pineapple and orange juice. Chill until syrupy.

Fold in apricots, pineapple and marshmallows. Pour into 9 x 9 inch (22 x 22 cm) pan. Chill. Serve with fruit dressing and rolls or baking powder biscuits. Serves 9-12.

FRUIT DRESSING

All purpose flour	2 tbsp.	30 mL
Granulated sugar	½ cup	125 mL
Beaten egg	1	1
Orange juice	½ cup	125 mL
Apricot, pineapple and orange juice (reserved)	½ cup	125 mL
Butter or margarine	1 tbsp.	15 mL
Whipping cream (or 1 envelope topping)	1 cup	250 mL

In top of double boiler stir flour and sugar together well. Stir in beaten egg. Add juices. Cook over boiling water stirring frequently until thickened. Stir in butter. Cool.

Whip cream until stiff. Fold into cooled dressing. Spoon over individual servings of salad.

Pare Pointer

Opportunities always look bigger going away than coming.

BANANA ORANGE SALAD

Extra good. Sure to be the show-off of any buffet table. Delicate banana. Great orange flavor.

Orange-flavored gelatin	1 – 3 oz.	1 – 85 g
Boiling water	1 cup	225 mL
Frozen orange juice (undiluted)	¾ cup	175 mL
Granulated sugar	½ cup	125 mL
Cream cheese, softened	4 oz.	125 g
Crushed pineapple, drained	14 oz.	398 mL
Mashed bananas	2	2
Orange segments, drained	10 oz.	284 mL
Whipping cream (or 1 envelope topping)	1 cup	250 mL

Put gelatin and boiling water in saucepan. Stir to dissolve. Add orange juice and sugar. Heat and stir over low heat to dissolve sugar. Remove from heat.

Mash cream cheese together with drained pineapple. Add to jelly.

Add mashed banana and orange segments. Chill until syrupy.

Whip cream until stiff. Fold into thickened jelly. Pour into mold or serving bowl. Chill.

ORANGE CHEESE SALAD: Add 1 cup (250 mL) cottage cheese. No cottage cheese ever had it so good.

ORANGE TEA SALAD

Makes a pretty amber colored salad.

Orange-flavored gelatin	1 – 3 oz.	85 g
Hot tea, quite strong	1 cup	225 mL
Crushed pineapple with juice	1 cup	225 mL
Orange sections, drained	10 oz.	284 mL

Dissolve gelatin in hot tea.

Add pineapple and orange sections. Chill until syrupy. Pour into mold or glass bowl. Chill.

MANDARIN ORANGE SALAD

So refreshing and so quick to prepare.

Orange-flavored gelatin	1 – 3 oz.	1 – 85 g
Boiling water	1 cup	225 mL
Crushed pineapple with juice	14 oz.	398 mL
Mandarin orange sections, drained	10 oz.	284 mL
Salad dressing	1 tbsp.	15 mL

Combine gelatin with boiling water. Stir to dissolve. Add pineapple. Stir. Chill until slightly thickened stirring once or twice.

Fold orange sections and salad dressing into thickened jelly. Fold until salad dressing is blended. Pour into 3 cup (700 mL) mold. Chill.

DOUBLE ORANGE MOLD

Lots of orange in this simple recipe.

Orange-flavored gelatin	1 – 3 oz.	1 – 85 g
Boiling water	1 cup	225 mL
Frozen orange juice (undiluted)	¾ cup	150 mL
Orange sections, drained	10 oz.	284 mL
Pineapple bits, drained	14 oz.	398 mL

Mayonnaise for garnish.

Dissolve gelatin in boiling water. Stir in orange juice. Chill until syrupy.

Add orange sections and pineapple bits to thickened jelly. Pour into mold or bowl. Chill. Top with a dollop of mayonnaise to serve. Serves 6-8.

Pare Pointer

The main difficulty with a liar is the necessity of having a good memory.

FROSTY MARASCHINO NUT

Great eye appeal and greater taste.

Cream cheese, softened	4 oz.	125 g
Powdered sugar	¼ cup	50 mL
Mayonnaise	2 tbsp.	30 mL
Cherry juice	1 tbsp.	15 mL
Maraschino cherries, quartered	1 cup	250 mL
Chopped pecans or walnuts	1 cup	250 mL
Whipping cream (or 1 envelope topping)	1 cup	250 mL

Mash cream cheese and sugar. Add mayonnaise and cherry juice. Mix together well. May be a bit lumpy.

Stir in cherries and nuts.

Whip cream until stiff. Fold into salad. Put into muffin pans lined with paper cups or into soup cans. Freeze. Cover to store.

Note: A few drops of red food coloring may be added if a deeper shade is desired.

Pictured on page 107.

FROZEN MINT

A creamy mint delight.

Lime-flavored gelatin	1 – 3 oz.	1 – 85 g
Boiling water	1 cup	250 mL
Whipping cream	2 cups	500 mL
Peppermint flavoring	½ tsp.	3 mL
Small marshmallows	2 cups	500 mL

Dissolve gelatin in boiling water. Chill until syrupy.

Whip cream until stiff. Fold in peppermint flavoring and marshmallows. Fold into thickened jelly. Pour into ring mold, tube mold or muffin tins lined with paper cups. Freeze. Cover to store. Serves 8-10.

Pictured on page 107.

CRANBERRY FROZEN SALAD

Any luncheon would be a success with this.

Cream cheese, softened	4 oz.	125 g
Mayonnaise	2 tbsp.	30 mL
Powdered sugar	¼ cup	50 mL
Vanilla	1 tsp.	5 mL
Whole cranberry sauce	1 cup	250 mL
Crushed pineapple, drained	14 oz.	398 mL
Chopped walnuts	⅓ cup	75 mL
Whipping cream (or 1 envelope topping)	1 cup	250 mL

Combine cheese, mayonnaise, sugar and vanilla. Mash together well. May be a bit lumpy.

Stir in cranberry sauce, drained pineapple and nuts.

Whip cream until stiff. Fold into salad. Spoon into muffin tins (lined with paper cups) or cans. Freeze. Store frozen cups in container. Cover cans. To serve canned salad, open bottom end and push salad out onto plate. Slice just before serving. Serves 6-8.

FROZEN VELVET

When this begins to thaw you will marvel at its smoothness.

Cream cheese, softened	8 oz.	250 g
Mayonnaise	1 cup	250 mL
Powdered sugar	¼ cup	50 mL
Small marshmallows	2 cups	500 mL
Fruit cocktail, drained	14 oz.	398 mL
Maraschino cherries, quartered	8	8
Whipping cream (or 1 envelope topping)	1 cup	250 mL

Mash cream cheese in mixing bowl. Add mayonnaise and sugar. Beat to combine.

Stir in marshmallows, fruit cocktail and cherries.

Whip cream until stiff. Fold into fruit mixture. Spoon into mold, muffin cups, cans or ring mold. Freeze. Cover until required. Serves 10-12.

FRUIT FREEZE

Orange fruit nestled in a snowy background. Tasty.

Cream cheese, softened	**4 oz.**	**125 g**
Mayonnaise	**½ cup**	**125 mL**
Powdered sugar	**¼ cup**	**50 mL**
Apricots or peaches, drained, cut up	**14 oz.**	**398 mL**
Crushed pineapple, drained	**14 oz.**	**398 mL**
Small marshmallows	**1 cup**	**250 mL**
Whipping cream		
(or 1 envelope topping)	**1 cup**	**250 mL**
Chopped nuts (optional)	**¼ cup**	**50 mL**

Mash cream cheese. Add mayonnaise and sugar. Mix together well. It will be a little lumpy.

Stir in well drained apricots and pineapple. Mix in marshmallows.

Whip cream until stiff. Fold into fruit along with chopped nuts. Spoon into freezing containers, ring mold, muffin tins, loaf pan or soup cans. Freeze. Cover to store. Serves 8.

PINEAPPLE FROST: Omit apricots. Add 1 can drained orange segments, 10 oz. (284 mL).

Paré Pointer

If you have a narrow mind, education will broaden it but there is no cure for a big head.

So flavorful, such a pretty way to use a pie filling.

Cherry pie filling	19 oz.	540 mL
Crushed pineapple, well drained	14 oz.	398 mL
Condensed milk	10 oz.	284 mL
Lemon juice	3 tbsp.	45 mL
Almond flavoring	½ tsp.	3 mL
Whipping cream (or 2 envelopes topping)	2 cups	500 mL

Empty cherry pie filling into bowl. Stir in pineapple, condensed milk, lemon juice and almond.

Whip cream until stiff. Fold into cherry mixture. Spoon into muffin tins lined with paper cups or into soup cans. Freeze. Pack frozen salad cups into container to store. Cover soup cans to store. To serve from cans, remove bottom end, push through onto plate. Slice and serve. Serves 10-12.

Pictured on page 107.

FROZEN BLUSHING SALAD

A delicious make-a-long-time-ahead salad.

Cream cheese	8 oz.	250 g
Granulated sugar	⅓ cup	75 mL
Crushed pineapple with juice	1 cup	250 mL
Package frozen strawberries, thawed	10 oz.	284 g
Whipping cream (or 1 envelope topping)	1 cup	250 mL

Have cream cheese at room temperature. Add sugar and mix well to dissolve. Add pineapple and strawberries. Stir and mash with fork. It will be a bit lumpy.

Whip cream until stiff. Fold into fruit. Pour into ring mold or soup cans. Freeze. Cover to store. Unmold ring on plate. If in cans, remove bottom end and push salad out on plate. Slice. Serves 8-10.

FROST ON THE LEMON

Creamy and lemony — an excellent goodie. Do try it.

Lemon instant pudding powder (4 portion size)	1	1
Milk	1½ cups	375 mL
Mayonnaise	½ cup	125 mL
Lemon juice	2 tbsp.	30 mL
Fruit cocktail, drained	14 oz.	398 mL
Maraschino cherries, quartered	6	6
Small marshmallows	1 cup	250 mL
Whipping cream (or 1 envelope topping)	1 cup	250 mL

Put pudding powder into bowl. Add milk, mayonnaise and lemon juice. Beat to combine. Allow to thicken a few minutes.

Stir in drained fruit cocktail, cherries and marshmallows.

Whip cream until stiff. Fold into fruit mixture. Pour into soup cans, milk carton or muffin cups to freeze. Cover to store. Serves 10.

Pictured on page 107.

FROZEN STRAWBERRY SALAD

Pretty pink with a neat strawberry flavor.

Cream cheese	8 oz.	250 g.
Frozen strawberries, thawed	10 oz.	284 g
Whipping cream (or 1 envelope topping)	1 cup	250 mL

Have cream cheese at room temperature. Mash with fork. Add strawberries. Mash and stir until mixed together well. Mixture will be a bit lumpy.

Whip cream until stiff. Fold into berry mixture. Pour into cans or muffin tins lined with paper cups. Freeze. Cover when frozen until used. Serves 6-8.

FROZEN WALDORF

And it tastes like Waldorf salad too!

Granulated sugar	¼ cup	50 mL
All purpose flour	1 tbsp.	15 mL
Egg	1	1
Pineapple juice	½ cup	125 mL
Salt	¼ tsp.	1 mL
Eating apples, peeled and diced	2	2
Celery finely chopped	½ cup	125 mL
Chopped walnuts	½ cup	125 mL
Whipping cream (or 1 envelope topping)	1 cup	250 mL

In small saucepan mix together sugar and flour. Add egg. Stir until moistened. Stir in pineapple juice and salt. Cook and stir over medium heat until it boils and thickens. Remove from heat. Cool. This step may be hastened by setting saucepan in cold water. Stir often.

Add apples, celery and nuts to cooled mixture.

Whip cream until stiff. Fold into apple mixture. Pour into freezer molds, cups or tube. Cover to store. Serves 6-8.

HOT POTATO SALAD

Uses leftover or fresh potatoes.

Hot cooked potatoes, cubed or sliced	4 cups	1 L
Chopped onion	½ cup	125 mL
Butter or margarine	1 tbsp.	15 mL
Cooked ham, cubed	½ cup	125 mL
Salad dressing	½ cup	125 mL
Salt	1 tsp.	5 mL
Pepper	¼ tsp.	1 mL

Keep potatoes hot while preparing additional ingredients.

Combine onion and butter in frying pan. Fry slowly until limp and clear.

Stir in ham, salad dressing, salt and pepper. Heat through. Pour over potatoes. Toss and serve.

GERMAN MACARONI SALAD

Just the right tang. The bacon adds to the appeal.

Raw elbow macaroni	1 cup	250 mL
DRESSING		
Bacon slices	4	4
All purpose flour	2 tbsp.	30 mL
Water	1 cup	250 mL
Vinegar	¼ cup	50 mL
Granulated sugar	⅓ cup	75 mL
Salt	½ tsp.	2 mL
Pepper	⅛ tsp.	½ mL
Chopped celery	½ cup	125 mL
Sliced green onions	4	4

Cook macaroni according to package directions. Prepare dressing in the meantime.

Fry bacon until crisp. Remove and crumble. Set aside. Stir flour into bacon drippings. Add water and vinegar. Cook and stir until thickened. Stir in sugar, salt and pepper. Keep warm until macaroni is cooked.

Add bacon, celery and onions to vinegar-sugar mixture. Heat until heated through. Pour over well drained macaroni. Stir. Serve hot. Makes 4 servings.

Variation: Omit macaroni. Use ready cut spaghetti. Makes a neater looking salad.

1. Frozen Mint page 100
2. Frost On The Lemon page 104
3. Cherry Freeze page 103
4. Frosty Maraschino Nut page 100

HOT CHICKEN SALAD

Make this in a saucepan. Serve it with cheese melting all over.

Cooked chicken, cut up	2 cups	500 mL
Chopped celery	1 cup	250 mL
Grated onion	1 tbsp.	15 mL
Salad dressing	½ cup	125 mL
Chopped walnuts	¼ cup	50 mL
Salt	½ tsp.	2 mL
Water	2 tbsp.	30 mL
Grated Cheddar cheese	1 cup	250 mL

Measure chicken, celery, onion, salad dressing, nuts, salt and water into heavy saucepan. Heat through stirring now and then. When piping hot, turn into pretty bowl.

Sprinkle cheese over top immediately. Serves 4.

GERMAN POTATO SALAD

Nice to serve instead of the usual potatoes. Scrumptious.

Hot potatoes, cubed or sliced	6 cups	1.4 L
Bacon slices	6	6
Small onion, finely chopped	1	1
All purpose flour	2 tbsp.	30 mL
Vinegar	¼ cup	50 mL
Water	¾ cup	175 mL
Granulated sugar	2 tbsp.	30 mL
Dried parsley flakes	1 tsp.	5 mL
Salt	½ tsp.	2 mL
Pepper	⅛ tsp.	½ mL

Keep potatoes hot after cooking.

Fry bacon. Remove and crumble. Set aside.

Fry onion slowly in bacon fat until soft and clear. Stir in flour. Add vinegar and water. Stir until thickened. Stir in sugar, parsley, salt and pepper. You may need more salt and pepper. Add bacon. Pour over cubed potatoes. Toss and serve 6.

DRIED FRUIT COMPOTE

Great for a barbeque or buffet table. Unusual and delicious.

Dried mixed fruit, cut	12 oz.	340 g
Water	2 cups	500 mL
Granulated sugar	½ cup	125 mL
Raisins	¼ cup	50 mL
Juice from fruit plus water if needed	1 cup	250 mL
Lemon juice	1 tsp.	5 mL
Curry powder	1 tsp.	5 mL
Cold water	1 tbsp.	15 mL
Corn starch	1 tbsp.	15 mL

Cut dried apricots in half, peaches in quarters and pears in quarters. Combine with water, sugar and raisins in saucepan. Bring to boil. Simmer covered 15 minutes.

Measure juice from fruit into saucepan adding water if needed to make 1 cup (250 mL). Stir in lemon juice and curry powder. Heat to boiling.

Mix starch and water together in cup. Pour into hot juice while stirring. Boil to thicken. Combine with fruit. Serve hot.

Variation: Omit curry. Add ½ tsp. (2 mL) cinnamon. Gives a bit of a different flavor.

HOT ITALIAN SALAD

A great way to use leftover potatoes, or start with fresh.

Bacon slices, cooked and crumbled	6	6
Cooked potatoes, cubed	4 cups	1 L
Italian dressing	½ cup	125 mL
Green onions sliced	4-6	4-6
Chopped celery	½ cup	125 mL
Parmesan cheese	½ cup	125 mL

Fry bacon in large frying pan. Remove to crumble. Pour fat from pan. Return crumbled bacon to pan.

Add potatoes, dressing, onions and celery. Heat, stirring frequently, until heated through.

Spoon into serving bowl. Add cheese. Stir and serve.

BEST RICE SALAD

Do try this recipe. It is widely acclaimed.

Hot cooked rice	2 cups	500 mL
Chopped celery	1½ cups	375 mL
Peas, fresh or frozen	1 cup	250 mL
Green onions, finely chopped	¼ cup	50 mL
Can of small shrimp	4 oz.	113 g
Salad oil	½ cup	125 mL
Vinegar	3 tbsp.	50 mL
Soy sauce	2 tbsp.	30 mL
Curry powder	1½-2 tsp.	7-10 mL
Salt	1 tsp	5 mL
Granulated sugar	½ tsp.	2 mL
Monosodium glutamate	½ tsp.	2 mL
Celery salt	½ tsp.	2 mL

Put hot rice in bowl. Add celery, peas, onions and shrimp.

In small bowl mix next eight ingredients. Stir and pour over rice mixture. Stir lightly to coat. Serves 4-6.

PICKLED SHRIMP

This salad actually tastes better than it looks. Scrumptious.

Tins of shrimp (or fresh)	2–4 oz.	2–113 g
Chopped celery	1 cup	250 mL
Hard boiled eggs, chopped	3	3
Bread and butter pickles, quartered	½ cup	125 mL
Chopped walnuts	½ cup	125 mL
Mayonnaise	¼ cup	50 mL
Sprinkle of salt		
Sprinkle of pepper		

Rinse and drain shrimp. Combine in bowl with celery, eggs, pickles and nuts.

Spoon mayonnaise over shrimp mixture, adding a bit more if too dry. Sprinkle salt and pepper to taste. Serves 4-6.

Note: Sliced sweet pickles may be exchanged for the bread and butter pickles.

CARROT SEA SALAD

*This is one salad that you can't tell how good it is by reading the recipe.
You just have to make it.*

Carrots, grated	2 cups	500 mL
Celery, cut fine	1 cup	250 mL
Green onions, sliced	⅓ cup	75 mL
Mayonnaise	1 cup	250 mL
Salt, sprinkle		
Pepper, sprinkle		
Seasoned salt, sprinkle		
Cans of small shrimp	2 – 4 oz.	2 – 114 g
Shoestring potato chips	2 cups	500 mL

Peel carrots and shred. Put into small bowl. Add cut celery and onion.
Stir in mayonnaise, salt, pepper, and seasoned salt. Can be made
ahead to this point and refrigerated.

Shortly before serving, drain shrimp, rinse with cold water and drain
again. Combine gently with vegetables. Add potato chips. Toss and
serve. Makes 6 servings.

Variation: Omit green onions. Add 1 purple onion, sliced thin. Good!

SHRIMP SALAD

If you like olives you will appreciate this combination.

Tins of shrimp (or fresh)	2–4 oz.	2–113 g
Chopped celery	½ cup	125 mL
Sliced green onions (optional)	2 tbsp.	30 mL
Sliced pimento stuffed olives	½ cup	125 mL
Mayonnaise	¼ cup	50 mL
Sprinkle of salt		
Sprinkle of pepper		

Place rinsed and drained shrimp in bowl. Add celery, onions and olives.

Stir mayonnaise into shrimp mixture. Add salt and pepper to taste.
Serves 4.

PEPPERED SHRIMP: Omit olives. Add ½ cup (125 mL) chopped green
pepper.

LOBSTER NOODLE SALAD

A special company dish.

Can of lobster (or fresh)	5 oz.	142 g
Cooked alphabet noodles	2 cups	500 mL
Chopped celery	¼ cup	50 mL
Stuffed olives, sliced	3 tbsp.	50 mL
Green onions, thinly sliced	1 tbsp.	15 mL
Salt, sprinkle		
Mayonnaise	⅓ cup	75 mL
Cream or milk	1 tbsp.	15 mL
Lemon juice	1 tsp.	5 mL
Lettuce cups (or shredded)	4	4
Tomatoes in wedges	2	2
Salt and pepper, sprinkle		

Combine lobster, noodles, celery, olives and onions in bowl. Sprinkle with salt.

In small bowl mix mayonnaise, cream and lemon juice. Add to salad. Toss lightly.

Arrange lettuce on plates. Spoon lobster mixture over lettuce with tomato wedge for garnish. Sprinkle with salt and pepper. Serves 4.

CRABBY RICE SALAD

The rice blends right in. It is a good extender.

Can of crab (or fresh)	1 – 4¾ oz.	1 – 135 g
Cooked cold rice	1½ cups	350 mL
Chopped celery	¼ cup	50 mL
Parsley flakes	½ tsp.	2 mL
Olives, chopped or sliced	¼-½ cup	50-125 mL
Mayonnaise	2½ tbsp.	35 mL
Lettuce		

Combine first six ingredients in bowl. Mix together adding a bit more mayonnaise if needed. Serve over lettuce. Add salt if needed. Serves 4.

CRABBY CURRY SALAD: Add ½ tsp. (2 mL) curry to salad. Stir to mix.

LOBSTER SALAD

For that special luncheon.

Lobster, drained (or fresh)	2 – 5 oz.	2 – 142 g
Chopped celery	1 cup	250 mL
Hard boiled eggs, chopped	2	2
Mayonnaise	½ cup	125 mL
Lemon juice	2 tsp.	10 mL
Ketchup	1 tsp.	5 mL
Granulated sugar	½ tsp.	2 mL
Salt	¼ tsp.	1 mL
Shredded lettuce		
Parsley for garnish		
Tomato, cut in wedges		

Combine lobster, celery and eggs in bowl.

Mix next five dressing ingredients together well. Pour over lobster mixture. Mix.

Put lettuce on large serving plate or individual plates. Top with lobster mixture and garnish with tomato wedges and parsley. Serves 4-6.

SHRIMP PASTA SALAD

A main dish salad. Spaghetti ready cut is so much neater than macaroni.

Ready cut spaghetti (or macaroni)	2 cups	500 mL
Chopped celery (some leaves)	½ cup	125 mL
Tin of shrimp (or fresh)	4 oz.	113 g
Salad dressing	½ cup	125 mL
Seasoned salt	½ tsp.	2 mL
Salt sprinkle		
Pepper sprinkle		

Cook spaghetti according to directions on package. Drain. Cool.

Add celery, shrimp, dressing and seasoned salt. Stir to mix. Sprinkle salt and pepper. Toss and add more if needed. Chill until ready to serve. Serves 6.

Variation: Omit seasoned salt. Add ¼ tsp. (1 mL) garlic salt.

This main dish salad can be arranged to suit your fancy.

SALAD

Head lettuce, torn	1	1
Romaine lettuce, torn	1	1
Canned tuna	2 – 6½ oz.	2 – 184 g
Red onion, thinly sliced	1	1
Black olives, pitted, sliced	½ cup	125 mL
Celery, sliced thin	1 cup	250 mL
Cooked potatoes, sliced	4 med.	4 med.
Julienne green beans, drained	14 oz.	398 mL
Salad oil	½ cup	125 mL
Red wine vinegar	3 tbsp.	50 mL
Chopped parsley	¼ cup	50 mL
Lemon juice	1 tbsp.	15 mL
Salt	½ tsp.	2 mL
Pepper	¼ tsp.	1 mL
Garlic powder	¼ tsp.	1 mL
Tomatoes, cut in wedges	2	2
Hard boiled eggs, quartered	3	3
Anchovies for garnish (optional)		

Line large platter or salad bowl with lettuce.

Layer tuna, onion, olives, celery, potatoes and beans over top.

Mix salad oil, vinegar, parsley, lemon juice, salt, pepper and garlic powder together. Drizzle over salad.

Arrange tomato and egg wedges over or around salad. Make pattern with anchovies on top if using them. Use a few of the slices of olives to decorate top also.

Paré Pointer

He thinks a will of his own is not as good as the will of a rich relative.

MACARONI SHELL SALAD

Sea shells are a natural to combine with tuna.

Shell macaroni	2 cups	500 mL
Tuna, drained	7 oz.	198 g
Celery, sliced thin	½ cup	125 mL
Hard boiled eggs, quartered	2	2
Peeled cucumber, cubed	½ cup	125 mL
Cherry tomatoes		
(or large ones cut)	2 cups	500 mL
Salad dressing	½ cup	125 mL
Lemon juice	1 tbsp.	15 mL
Garlic salt	¼ tsp.	1 mL
Paprika	¼ tsp.	1 mL

Cook macaroni according to package directions. Drain well. Cool.

Add tuna, breaking up chunks. Add celery, eggs, cucumber and tomatoes. Add salt if needed.

Mix salad dressing with lemon juice, garlic salt and paprika. Spoon over top of salad. Mix very lightly. Serves 6.

SALMON LUNCHEON SALAD

An economical fish salad.

Tins of salmon	2 – 7¾ oz.	2 – 220 g
Chopped celery	½ cup	125 mL
Sweet pickle relish	½ cup	125 mL
Chopped green pepper	2 tbsp.	30 mL
Mayonnaise	⅓ cup	75 mL
Lemon juice	1 tbsp.	15 mL
Salt	½ tsp.	2 mL
Lettuce		

Drain salmon. Remove round bones and black skin if any. Break up large pieces. Add celery, relish and green pepper.

Stir mayonnaise, lemon juice and salt together. Add to salmon mixture. Stir lightly to distribute.

Serve on shredded lettuce or lettuce cups. Serves 6.

POLYNESIAN SHRIMP SALAD

Easy to add more curry if you find this too mild.

Tins of shrimp (or fresh)	2–4 oz.	2–113 g
Chopped celery	2 cups	500 mL
Water chestnuts, sliced	1 – 10 oz.	1 – 284 mL
Fresh bean sprouts	1 cup	250 mL
Sliced green onions	2	2
Mayonnaise	¼ cup	50 mL
Curry powder	¼ tsp.	1 mL
Salt	⅛ tsp.	½ mL

Put rinsed and drained shrimp in bowl. Add celery, water chestnuts, sprouts and onions.

Mix mayonnaise, curry powder and salt together in small bowl. Spoon over shrimp mixture. Toss to coat. Serves 4.

CRAB CHEESE SALAD

This has a cream cheese dressing.

Tinned crab (or fresh)	4¾ oz.	135 g
Chopped celery	¼ cup	50 mL
Cream cheese, softened	4 oz.	125 g
Mayonnaise	2 tbsp.	30 mL
Lemon juice	4 tsp.	20 mL
Onion salt	¼ tsp.	1 mL
Lettuce, torn or shredded	2 cups	500 mL

Combine crab and celery in bowl.

Mash cream cheese with fork on plate. Add mayonnaise, lemon juice and onion salt. Mash well. Add to crab mixture.

Serve over lettuce or add lettuce to salad and toss. Serves 4.

PACKAGED MACARONI SALAD

One of the best salads right from the shelf. So easy.

Package of macaroni and cheese	8 oz.	225 g
Cut green beans, drained	14 oz.	398 mL
Tiny peas, drained	14 oz.	398 mL
Tuna, drained and broken up	6½ oz.	184 g
Salad dressing	½ cup	125 mL

Prepare macaroni and cheese as directed on package. Cool.

Add beans, peas and tuna to cooled macaroni.

Add enough salad dressing to moisten. Amount given is approximate. Serves 8-10.

CRABBY TOSS

It's a toss up whether or not to double it.

Lettuce, cut bite size	2 cups	500 mL
Cucumber, diced	½ cup	125 mL
Celery, diced	½ cup	125 mL
Green onions, sliced	2	2
Tin of crab (or fresh)	4¾ oz.	135 g
Salad dressing	½ cup	125 mL
Ketchup	1 tbsp.	15 mL
Worcestershire sauce	1 tsp.	5 mL
Lemon juice	1 tsp.	5 mL
Salt	½ tsp.	2 mL
Pepper	¼ tsp.	1 mL

Combine first five ingredients together in bowl.

Mix salad dressing with ketchup in small bowl. Add Worcestershire sauce, lemon juice, salt and pepper. Stir. Add to crab mixture. Toss. Serves 4.

A lunch in itself when accompanied by a dinner roll or better yet, the Irish Brown Bread in Company's Coming — Muffins & More.

LOUIS DRESSING

Mayonnaise	½ cup	125 mL
Chili sauce	¼ cup	50 mL
Dry onion flakes	1 tsp.	5 mL
Cream or milk	1 tbsp.	15 mL
French dressing	2 tbsp.	30 mL
Worcestershire sauce	½ tsp.	2 mL

Mix all six ingredients together in bowl.

SALAD

Small firm head of lettuce	1	1
Tins of crab (or fresh)	2–5 oz.	2–142 g
Hard boiled eggs	4	4
Tomatoes	2	2

Cut or tear lettuce. Pile in center of individual salad plates or in center of platter. Drain crab. Put over top of lettuce, tossing it together a bit. Cut eggs lengthwise into quarters. Arrange around outside edge of lettuce. Cut tomatoes in wedges. Arrange around outside edge of lettuce also. Spoon some of the dressing over the lettuce-crab combination. Serve rest of dressing in a separate bowl. Serves 4-6.

Note: Try this by omitting from the dressing ½ tsp. (2 mL) Worcestershire sauce and 2 tbsp. (30 mL) French dressing. It is a bit milder and a pretty pink color.

SHRIMP LOUIS: Omit crab. Add same amount of shrimp, fresh or canned.

Pictured on page 125.

Don't touch that money. It is tainted. Taint yours. Taint mine.

SCANDINAVIAN SALAD

This has a mild dressing. All the better for salad flavor to come through.

Crabmeat, canned or fresh	2 cups	500 mL
Cooked potatoes, diced	2 cups	500 mL
Hard boiled eggs, chopped	2	2
Diced apples	2	2
Raisins	1 cup	250 mL
Chopped green pepper	½ cup	125 mL
Chopped celery	½ cup	125 mL
Minced onion	1 tbsp.	15 mL
Salt sprinkle		
Pepper sprinkle		
Whipping cream (or topping)	½ cup	125 mL
Mayonnaise	1 cup	250 mL
Lemon juice	1 tsp.	5 mL

Measure first ten ingredients in bowl.

Whip cream until stiff. Add mayonnaise and lemon juice. Fold in. Add and toss with salad or serve on the side. Serves 6-8.

SHRIMP NEPTUNE

A showy appetizing salad. A winner.

Tin of shrimp (or fresh)	1 – 4 oz.	1 – 113 g
Frozen peas, cooked	1 cup	250 mL
Chopped celery	1 cup	250 mL
Hard boiled eggs	3	3
Cheddar cheese, cut in strips	⅓ cup	75 mL
Salad dressing	½ cup	125 mL
Salt	½ tsp.	2 mL
Worcestershire sauce	½ tsp.	2 mL

Drain shrimp. Rinse and drain again. Place in bowl. Add peas, celery, eggs and cheese.

In a small bowl mix salad dressing, salt and Worcestershire sauce. Pour over shrimp mixture. Toss to coat. Serves 4.

TUNA SALAD

A chicken of the sea salad.

Canned tuna, drained	7 oz.	198 g
Cucumber, diced	½ cup	125 mL
Celery, thinly sliced	¼ cup	50 mL
Green onion, sliced	1	1
Salad dressing	3-4 tsp.	15–20 mL
Lettuce		
Hard boiled eggs	2	2

Put tuna, cucumber, celery and onion in bowl. Add salad dressing and stir lightly to combine.

Serve on lettuce. Arrange egg slices around salad. Add salt if needed. Serves 4.

CRAB CELERY SALAD

Crusty rolls and salad. Just right.

Canned crab (or fresh)	4¾ oz.	135 g
Sliced celery	½ cup	125 mL
Hard boiled eggs, chopped	2	2
Salt	½ tsp.	2 mL
Mayonnaise	¼ cup	50 mL
Lemon juice	1 tsp.	5 mL
Lettuce, shredded	2 cups	500 mL

Combine crab, celery, eggs and salt in bowl.

Mix mayonnaise with lemon juice. Add to salad. Stir lightly to mix.

Spoon salad over lettuce or instead, toss lettuce with salad. Serves 4.

DILLED BEEF SALAD

With crusty roll, this is a good lunch. Has a creamy mustard sauce.

Roast beef, cut in strips	2 cups	500 mL
Celery, sliced thin	½ cup	125 mL
Red bell pepper, cut in strips	1	1
Dill pickle, medium, cut up	1	1
Green onions, sliced	2	2
Salt sprinkle		
Egg yolk	1	1
Vinegar	1 tbsp.	15 mL
Prepared mustard	1 tsp.	5 mL
Horseradish (or to taste)	½ tsp.	2 mL
Salad oil	⅓ cup	75 mL

Measure beef, celery, red pepper, dill pickle, onions and salt into bowl. Set aside.

Beat egg yolk with a fork or whisk in small bowl. Beat in vinegar, mustard and horseradish.

Beat in oil very gradually until thick. Add half to beef mixture. Toss. Add more dressing as needed. Serves 4.

DEVILLED EGGS

These eggs do double duty. They can also be used as an appetizer.

Hard boiled eggs, peeled	6	6
Salad dressing	¼ cup	50 mL
Dry mustard	½ tsp.	2 mL
Salt	½ tsp.	2 mL
Pepper	⅛ tsp.	½ mL
Paprika		

Cut eggs in half lengthwise. Put yolks on plate. Add salad dressing, mustard, salt and pepper. Mash with fork until smooth and mixed well. If too dry, add a bit of milk. Fill egg white halves. A pastry tube will give an artistic design.

Sprinkle with paprika. Serves 6.

Note: If using cooked salad dressing on page 135, omit mustard.

CHICKEN MOLD

You get both the chicken and the egg with this salad.

Unflavored gelatin powders	2 – ¼ oz.	2 – 7 g
Cold water	½ cup	125 mL
Hot water	1½ cups	350 mL
Chicken cubes	2	2
Cooked chicken, cubed	1½ cups	350 mL
Chopped celery	¾ cup	175 mL
Chopped pimento	2 tbsp.	30 mL
Chopped onion	2 tbsp.	30 mL
Lemon juice	2 tsp.	10 mL
Salt, sprinkle		
Hard boiled eggs, sliced	2	2

Sprinkle gelatin over cold water. Let stand 5 minutes.

In small saucepan stir hot water and chicken cubes. Stir until melted. Add gelatin. Stir until dissolved. Chill until syrupy.

Add chicken, celery, pimento, onion, lemon juice and salt. Stir. Transfer to 8 × 8 inch (20 × 20 cm) pan. Arrange egg slices over top, being careful to push them just below surface of gelatin. Chill. Serves 9.

EGG SALAD

Use up those extra eggs.

Hard boiled eggs, chopped	8	8
Diced celery	1 cup	250 mL
Sweet pickle relish	¼ cup	50 mL
Mayonnaise	½ cup	125 mL
Lemon juice	1 tbsp.	15 mL
Worcestershire sauce	½ tsp.	2 mL
Onion flakes (or minced fresh)	½ tsp	2 mL
Parsley flakes	½ tsp.	2 mL
Salt	½ tsp.	2 mL
Pepper	⅛ tsp.	½ mL

Put chopped eggs into bowl. Add celery and relish. Set aside.

In small bowl measure in remaining seven ingredients. Stir well until blended. Pour over egg mixture. Stir lightly. Serves 6-8.

CHEF'S SALAD

A meal in itself when accompanied by crusty rolls.

Head of lettuce, torn or cut	1	1
Red onion, sliced (optional)	1	1
Cucumber, peeled or scored, cut up	½	½
Green onions, sliced	4	4
Edam cheese, cut in strips (or Swiss)	1 cup	250 mL
Chicken or turkey, cut in strips	1 cup	250 mL
Ham, cut in strips	1 cup	250 mL
Radish, thinly sliced (optional)	½ cup	125 mL
Tomatoes, cut in wedges	2	2
Hard cooked eggs, cut in wedges	3	3

Tear or cut lettuce into bowl or single serving bowls.

Add next seven ingredients to lettuce being sure to save enough of each item for garnish. Arrange over top of salad in attractive design. Serve with your favorite dressing.

Garnish with tomato wedges and hard cooked eggs.

CHEF'S COLD CUT SALAD: Omit chicken and ham. Add cubed salami and bologna.

Note: Adding half romaine lettuce or other greens gives more interest to the salad.

1. Crab Louis page 119
2. Louis Dressing page 119

CHICKEN BOWL SALAD

Very tasty. An excellent use of left-overs. You may want to add more hot pepper sauce.

Cooked chicken, cubed	2 cups	500 mL
Thinly sliced celery	1 cup	250 mL
Pineapple bits	1 cup	250 mL
Slivered almonds, toasted	¼ cup	50 mL
Sprinkle of salt		
Mayonnaise	½ cup	125 mL
Pineapple juice	¼ cup	50 mL
Hot pepper sauce	½ tsp.	3 mL
Avocados	2-3	2-3
Lettuce for serving		

Combine chicken, celery, pineapple, almonds and salt in bowl.

In small bowl mix mayonnaise, pineapple juice and pepper sauce. Stir. Pour over salad. Toss lightly.

Halve avocados. Remove seed. Fill with salad. Arrange on lettuce. Serves 4-6.

SECOND DRESSING

A good variation for this salad.

Sour cream	¾ cup	175 mL
Lemon juice	1 tsp.	5 mL
Curry powder	½ tsp.	2 mL
Salt	½ tsp.	2 mL

Mix all together. Toss with salad. Pile into avocado shells.

Note: Toast almonds in 350°F (180°C) oven for 5 minutes until golden.

Fare Pointer

Little Susie washed in Tide because it was too cold to wash out–tide.

BEEF SALAD

This zippy mustard dressing tones up any leftover beef.

Beef, cut in strips or cubes	2 cups	500 mL
Sliced celery	1 cup	250 mL
Tomato, cut in bite size pieces	1	1
Sliced green onions	2	2
Salad oil	1 tbsp.	15 mL
Vinegar	1 tbsp.	15 mL
Granulated sugar (optional)	1 tsp.	5 mL
Prepared mustard	1 tsp.	5 mL
Salt	½ tsp.	2 mL
Pepper	⅛ tsp.	½ mL
Lettuce		

Combine beef with celery, tomato and green onions.

Mix salad oil, vinegar and sugar in small bowl. Add mustard, salt and pepper. Stir. Add to beef mixture. Mix lightly.

Serve on shredded lettuce.

BEEF ONION SALAD

Leftover beef fits right in with this tasty piquant dressing.

Cooked beef cut in strips	2 cups	500 mL
Sliced mild onion	1	1
Cooked green beans	1 cup	250 mL
Salad oil	2 tbsp.	30 mL
Lemon juice	2 tbsp.	30 mL
Sugar (optional)	1 tsp.	5 mL
Garlic powder	⅛ tsp.	½ mL
Salt	¾ tsp.	3 mL
Pepper	¼ tsp.	1 mL
Torn lettuce		

Put beef, onion and beans into bowl.

Combine next six ingredients in small bowl. Pour over beef and onion. Stir lightly to combine.

Serve over torn lettuce. Serves 3-4.

CREAM CHICKEN SALAD

No mayonnaise in this recipe.

Chopped cooked chicken	2 cups	500 mL
Chopped celery	2 cups	500 mL
Chopped walnuts	¼ cup	50 mL
Sliced almonds	¼ cup	50 mL
Salt sprinkle		
Whipped cream (or topping)	½ cup	125 mL
Powdered sugar	1 tsp.	5 mL
Prepared mustard	1 tsp.	5 mL
Cayenne pepper	⅛ tsp.	½ mL
Lemon juice	1 tbsp.	15 mL
Lettuce cups		

Combine chicken, celery, walnuts, almonds and salt in bowl.

Combine whipped cream with sugar, mustard, cayenne and lemon juice. Add to chicken mixture. Toss. Check to see if a bit of salt is needed.

Serve in lettuce cups. Serves 4.

CHICKEN LUNCH SALAD

This never fails to please, with its darkish dressing.

Cooked chicken, cubed	2 cups	500 mL
Sliced celery	½ cup	125 mL
Green pepper, cut in strips	¼ cup	50 mL
Sliced olives or chopped pimento	2 tbsp.	30 mL
Mayonnaise	½ cup	125 mL
Minced onion	2 tbsp.	30 mL
Worcestershire sauce	2 tsp.	10 mL
Salt	¾ tsp.	3 mL
Pepper	¼ tsp.	1 mL

Measure chicken, celery, green pepper and olives into bowl.

In small bowl put mayonnaise, onion, Worcestershire sauce, salt and pepper. Mix together well. Pour over chicken mixture. Toss to coat. Serves 4.

COBB SALAD

A contribution to the salad world from California. Try your flair for arranging vegetables. An uncommon recipe. Not as complicated as it looks.

Medium head lettuce, shredded	1	1
Water cress, cut and stems off	1 cup	250 mL
Hard boiled eggs, divided, grated	3	3
Green onions, sliced	4	4
Bacon slices, cooked and crumbled	8	8
Cooked chicken, cubed	2½ cups	600 mL
Large tomato, chopped fine	1	1
Avocado, diced small	1	1

DRESSING

Vinegar	⅓ cup	75 mL
Salt	1 tsp.	5 mL
Pepper	¼ tsp.	2 mL
Dry mustard	½ tsp.	2 mL
Granulated sugar	½ tsp.	2 mL
Garlic powder	⅛ tsp.	½ mL
Salad oil	⅔ cup	150 mL
Blue cheese, crumbled	¼ cup	50 mL

Combine lettuce and watercress in large salad bowl. Add about one quarter of dressing. Toss to coat.

Remove yolks and grate. Also grate whites separately. Arrange yolks in center of bowl, and surround with whites. Make separate wedges of onions, bacon, chicken, tomato and avocado or mix these five together and pile around egg center. Serve with rest of dressing. Serves 4-6.

Note: You may prefer to make a wedge of crumbled blue cheese rather than add it to the dressing. You could also serve the lettuce on the side.

Pictured on page 143.

Paré Pointer

A buccaneer is far too high a price to pay for corn.

THREE C SALAD

Cream cheese chicken is delicious in lettuce cups or better yet, in stuffed tomatoes.

Crushed pineapple, drained (reserve juice)	1 cup	250 mL
Cooked chicken, cubed	2 cups	500 mL
Water chestnuts, drained and sliced	10 oz.	284 mL
Celery, sliced thin	½ cup	125 mL
Green onions, sliced	¼ cup	50 mL
Slivered almonds, toasted	¼ cup	50 mL
Salt	¼ tsp.	1 mL
Pepper, sprinkle		
Cream cheese, softened	8 oz.	250 g

Combine all first eight ingredients in bowl.

Mash cream cheese well. Gradually mix in all pineapple juice until blended. Pour over chicken mixture. Stir lightly.

Note: Toast almonds in 350°F (180°c) oven for 5 minutes until golden.

HAM LUNCH SALAD

The tangy dressing does this up proud.

Ham, chopped fine	2 cups	500 mL
Grated Swiss cheese	¾ cup	175 mL
Cooked peas, fresh or frozen	¾ cup	175 mL
Sweet pickle relish	1 tbsp.	15 mL
Prepared mustard	1 tsp.	5 mL
Salad dressing	¼ cup	50 mL
Milk	1 tbsp.	15 mL

Combine ham, cheese and peas in bowl.

In small bowl mix relish, mustard, salad dressing and milk. Stir and pour over ham mixture. Toss gently to coat adding more dressing if needed. Serves 4.

JAPANESE CHICKEN SALAD

Fantastic for lunch accompanied with hot, crusty rolls. Make it the night before and be ready for compliments.

Sesame seeds, toasted	2 tbsp.	30 mL
Slivered almonds, toasted	½ cup	125 mL
Cooked chicken, cubed	2 cups	500 mL
Small head of cabbage, shredded	1	1
Instant chicken noodles, crumbled (See Note)	3 oz.	85 g
Chopped green onions	2	2

DRESSING

Package of noodle seasoning	1	1
Salad oil	½ cup	125 mL
Vinegar	3 tbsp.	50 mL
Granulated sugar	1 tbsp.	15 mL
Monosodium glutamate	1 tsp.	5 mL
Salt	1 tsp.	5 mL
Pepper	½ tsp.	2 mL

Put sesame seeds and almonds in single layer in pan. Toast in 350°F (180°C) oven for 5 minutes or so until golden. Watch carefully after 5 minutes so they don't get too brown. Remove from oven. Set aside.

Put chicken into large bowl. Add cabbage, crumbled noodles and onions.

In small bowl combine packet of seasoning, oil, vinegar, sugar, mono-sodium glutamate, salt and pepper. Stir together. Pour over chicken-cabbage mixture. Stir. Store in covered bowl overnight in refrigerator to marinate. Just before serving sprinkle with sesame seeds and slivered almonds. Toss lightly to distribute. Serves 6.

Note: The instant chicken noodles come in 3 oz. (85 g) packages. They can be found in the soup section of grocery stores. There are Japanese, Chinese and other brands.

Pictured on cover.

Just made for a party! Fluffy pink dressing with a mild onion and curry flavor. Different and delicious.

Butter or margarine	2 tbsp.	30 mL
Large onion, chopped	1	1
Tomato paste	2 tbsp.	30 mL
Apricot jam	2 tbsp.	30 mL
Curry powder	½ tsp.	2 mL
Mayonnaise	½ cup	125 mL
Whipping cream (or topping)	½ cup	125 mL
Cooked chicken, cut bite size	3 cups	700 mL

Combine butter and chopped onion in frying pan. Fry until clear and soft.

Add tomato paste, jam and curry powder. Stir until melted in with onions. Remove from heat. Cool.

Add mayonnaise to cooled onion mixture. Whip cream until stiff. Fold into onion mixture. Add chicken. Toss lightly. Serve in pretty bowl.

BEEF SLAW

Have your meat and coleslaw all in one.

Cooked beef, cubed	2 cups	500 mL
Chopped celery	½ cup	125 mL
Shredded cabbage	1 cup	250 mL
Chopped dill pickle	¼ cup	50 mL
Salt, sprinkle		
Pepper, sprinkle		
Salad dressing	¼ cup	50 mL
Shredded lettuce		
Hard boiled eggs, sliced	3	3

Put beef, celery and cabbage in bowl. Add dill pickle and sprinkle with salt and pepper.

Add salad dressing. Mix well.

Serve over lettuce. Garnish with egg slices. Serves 3-4.

LAMB SALAD: Omit beef. Add 2 cups (500 mL) cooked cubed lamb.

CHICKEN PINEAPPLE

Short and sweet. Onion may be cut in rings.

Cooked chicken, cut up	2 cups	500 mL
Pineapple bits	½ cup	125 mL
Chopped onion, purple or green	¼ cup	50 mL
Salad dressing	¼ cup	50 mL
Salt	½ tsp.	2 mL
Pepper	⅛ tsp.	½ mL
Lettuce cups or shredded		

Combine chicken, pineapple and onion in bowl.

Add salad dressing, salt and pepper. Stir lightly to coat. Pile over lettuce. Serves 3-4.

HAM SALAD

Makes an attractive luncheon dish with its pink dressing.

Ham, cut in cubes	2 cups	500 mL
Sliced celery	1½ cups	375 mL
Tomato, chopped	1	1
Salt	¼ tsp.	1 mL
Salad dressing	⅓ cup	75 mL
Chili sauce	2 tbsp.	30 mL
Lettuce		
Hard boiled eggs for garnish	2	2

Combine ham, celery, tomato and salt in bowl.

Mix salad dressing with chili sauce. Pour over ham. Toss to coat. Pile on plate covered with lettuce. Garnish with egg sections.

CHICKEN EGG SALAD: Omit ham. Add 2 cups (500 mL) cubed, cooked chicken, ½ tsp. (2 mL) salt and ⅛ tsp. (½ mL) pepper.

COOKED SALAD DRESSING

From a way, way back. This has a lot of zip to it. A little goes a long way.

Granulated sugar	½ cup	125 mL
All purpose flour	2 tbsp.	30 mL
Dry mustard	1 tbsp.	15 mL
Salt	1 tsp.	5 mL
Eggs	3	3
Milk	1 cup	250 mL
Vinegar	½ cup	125 mL
Water	½ cup	125 mL

In top of double boiler put sugar, flour, mustard and salt. Stir until flour is thoroughly mixed in. Beat in eggs with a spoon one at a time.

Stir in milk, vinegar and water. Cook over boiling water stirring frequently until thickened. Pour into container. Store covered in refrigerator.

FOR LETTUCE SALADS: Thin dressing with a bit of milk or cream. Stir in about ½ tsp. (2 mL) granulated sugar for each four servings. Go by taste.

FOR DEVILLED EGGS: Use dressing straight from container. Add salt and pepper according to the number of eggs.

FOR POTATO SALAD: Thin dressing with a bit of milk or cream. No extra mustard or vinegar required.

FOR SANDWICHES: Use from container unless milk is needed to overcome dryness of sandwich filling. Gives new life to the same tired old sandwiches.

QUICK THOUSAND ISLAND

Nothing could be quicker to mix and serve over your bowl of greens.

Mayonnaise	1¼ cups	275 mL
Chili sauce or ketchup	½ cup	125 mL
Sweet pickle relish	¼ cup	50 mL
Dry onion flakes	1 tsp.	5 mL

Combine all four ingredients in small bowl. Mix together well. Makes 2 cups (500 mL).

CHEDDAR CHEESE DRESSING

Excellent to dress spinach salad or any other as well.

Eggs	2	2
Brown sugar	2 tsp.	10 mL
Salt	1½ tsp.	7 mL
Dry mustard	1 tsp.	5 mL
Worcestershire sauce	1 tsp.	5 mL
Horseradish	1 tsp.	5 mL
Salad oil	½ cup	125 mL
Vinegar	¼ cup	50 mL
Lemon juice	¼ cup	50 mL
Salad oil	1½ cups	375 mL
Cheddar cheese, grated	¼ lb.	115 g
Green onions, chopped fine	3	3

Combine first six ingredients in mixing bowl. Beat together well.

Add first amount of oil gradually, beating steadily.

Beat vinegar and lemon juice alternately with second amount of oil drizzled in. Beat 2-3 minutes. Transfer to blender. Beat until creamy, about 15 seconds. Pour into bowl.

Add cheese and onions. Stir. Store in refrigerator.

THOUSAND ISLAND

Put a ladle in a bowl of this dressing and let guests help themselves. The best!

Mayonnaise	2¼ cups	550 mL
Chili sauce	1 cup	250 mL
Sweet pickle relish	½ cup	125 mL
Finely chopped onion	2 tbsp.	30 mL
Hard boiled eggs	3	3
Chopped pimento	2 tbsp.	30 mL

Mix the mayonnaise, chili sauce, relish and onion together well.

Chop eggs quite fine. Add to mayonnaise mixture along with pimento. Store in refrigerator. Makes 4 cups (1L).

COTTAGE CHEESE TOPPING

Jazz up the cottage cheese to top off a fruit salad.

Cream cheese	4 oz.	125 g
Cottage cheese	1 cup	250 mL
Icing (confectioners) sugar	2 tbsp.	30 mL
Orange juice	2 tbsp.	30 mL
Lemon juice	2 tsp.	10 mL

Have cream cheese at room temperature. Mash together with cottage cheese. Mix in icing sugar, orange juice and lemon juice. Spoon over fresh fruit salad. Makes 1¾ cups (425 mL).

INSTANT LEMON TOPPING

And it is almost instant.

Lemon instant pudding powder,		
(4 portion size)	1	1
Milk	1 cup	225 mL
Whipping cream		
(or 1 envelope topping)	1 cup	250 mL

Put pudding powder, milk and cream into bowl. Beat until stiff. For jellied or fruit salads.

CREAM CHEESE DRESSING

Yet another yummy cream cheese topping.

Cream cheese	4 oz.	125 g
Icing (confectioners) sugar	2 tbsp.	30 mL
Cream or milk	1 tbsp.	15 mL
Vanilla	½ tsp.	2 mL

Have cream cheese at room temperature. Beat all four ingredients together well. Spread over flat surfaced jelly or spoon over separate servings. Serve also with fresh fruit.

OIL AND VINEGAR DRESSING

Such a simple recipe and also one of the most requested. It is better to add oil and vinegar separately to avoid the oil (which stays at the top) all coming out with the very first pouring. Very economical. A life saver for lettuce.

Vinegar	3 cups	750 mL
Granulated sugar	4 cups	1L

Salad oil as needed to serve

Combine vinegar and sugar in container. Stir, stir and stir! It will eventually dissolve. Store in cool place. Will keep for months. To use, pour equal amounts of oil and vinegar-sugar dressing over salad and toss. Oil may be cut down if desired. You will know when you have enough dressing. Too much and it will sink to the bottom of the bowl. Don't sprinkle salt over salad as it takes away the tartness of the dressing.

Note: This is especially good for help-yourself service. It speeds up the traffic through the food line compared to having separate bottles of dressings from which to choose.

BLUE CHEESE DRESSING

Jazz up the mayonnaise.

Mayonnaise	1 cup	250 mL
Blue cheese, crumbled	4 oz.	125 g
Dry onion flakes	1 tsp.	5 mL
Lemon juice	1 tbsp.	15 mL
Granulated sugar	1 tbsp.	15 mL

Mix all ingredients together. For a smooth dressing, purée in blender. Chill. Makes 1⅓ cups (375 mL).

MAYONNAISE

Try your own. Its goodness will surprise you.

Egg yolks	2	2
Dry mustard	1 tsp.	5 mL
Salt	1 tsp.	5 mL
Granulated sugar	1 tbsp.	15 mL
Cayenne pepper	⅛ tsp.	½ mL
Salad oil	¼ cup	50 mL
Vinegar	2-4 tbsp.	30-60 mL
Salad oil	1¾ cups	400 mL
Water	1 tbsp.	15 mL

Put yolks, mustard, salt, sugar and cayenne pepper into small mixing bowl. Beat to mix thoroughly at speed used to whip cream.

Still beating, add first amount of salad oil ¼ tsp. (1 mL) at a time. If mixture separates, begin again with 1 egg yolk and add mixture to it slowly as you beat until you reach the same place. Continue to add oil until ¼ cup (50 mL) is beaten in and thickened.

Beat in 1 Tbsp. (15 mL) vinegar and second amount of oil by adding in a thin stream. Use more vinegar as needed for thinning.

Beat in water last. Makes 2½ cups (625 mL).

PINK DRESSING

Good over anything.

Mayonnaise	1 cup	250 mL
Granulated sugar	¼ cup	50 mL
Walnuts	¼ cup	50 mL
Pineapple bits, drained	½ cup	125 mL
Cherry juice	¼ cup	50 mL
Maraschino cherries, chopped	¼ cup	50 mL
Whipping cream (or topping)	¼ cup	50 mL

Measure first six ingredients into blender. Blend until smooth. Pour into bowl.

Whip cream until stiff. Fold into dressing. Serve.

LEMON DRESSING

A delicious topping. Extra good.

Egg, beaten	1	1
Granulated sugar	¼ cup	50 mL
Lemon juice	¼ cup	50 mL
Whipping cream (or 1 envelope topping)	1 cup	250 mL

Beat egg in saucepan. Add sugar and lemon juice. Bring to boil stirring. Remove from heat. Cool.

Whip cream until stiff. Fold into cooled lemon mixture. Spoon over your favorite salad — jellied or fruit.

TARTAR SAUCE

Seafood dressing is so easy to make.

Mayonnaise	1 cup	250 mL
Chopped dill or sweet pickle	2 tbsp.	30 mL
Lemon juice	2 tbsp.	30 mL
Finely chopped celery	1 tbsp.	15 mL
Parsley flakes	1 tsp.	5 mL
Onion flakes	¼ tsp.	1 mL

Measure all six ingredients into small bowl. Mix together well. Store in refrigerator. Makes 1⅓ cups (325 mL).

FRUIT TOPPING

Serve over a fruit salad or use as a fruit dip.

Cream cheese	4 oz.	125 g
Sour cream	¼ cup	50 mL
Orange juice	2 tbsp.	30 mL
Icing (confectioners) sugar	2 tbsp.	30 mL
Lemon juice	1 tsp.	5 mL

Combine softened cream cheese with sour cream. Add orange juice and icing sugar. Beat together adding lemon juice. If stronger flavor is desired, add another 1 tsp. (5 mL) lemon juice. Makes a scant cupful.

FRENCH CREAM DRESSING

About the tastiest you will find. Super good.

Can of tomato soup	10 oz.	284 mL
Lemon juice	⅓ cup	75 mL
Honey	⅓ cup	75 mL
Vinegar	3 tbsp.	45 mL
Grated onion	2 tbsp.	30 mL
Worcestershire sauce	2 tsp.	10 mL
Prepared mustard	2 tsp.	10 mL
Salt	1½ tsp.	7 mL
Paprika	1 tsp.	5 mL
Celery seed	½ tsp.	2 mL
Garlic powder	¼ tsp.	1 mL
Salad oil	¾ cup	175 mL

Measure first eleven ingredients from tomato soup to garlic powder into small mixing bowl. Beat at medium speed for three minutes.

Add oil gradually, beating until all is blended in. Store in refrigerator. Makes 3 cups.

ITALIAN DRESSING

Great for marinating vegetables as well as for greens.

Salad oil	1 cup	225 mL
Lemon juice	¼ cup	50 mL
Vinegar	¼ cup	50 mL
Sugar	2 tsp.	10 mL
Salt	1 tsp.	5 mL
Dry mustard	½ tsp.	2 mL
Onion salt	½ tsp.	2 mL
Paprika	½ tsp.	2 mL
Oregano	½ tsp.	2 mL
Garlic salt (or 1 clove crushed)	½ tsp.	2 mL
Thyme	⅛ tsp.	½ mL

Measure all ingredients into jar. Cover. Shake well. Chill two hours before using.

STRAWBERRY DRESSING

Good on fruit salads and jellied salads.

Whipping cream	½ cup	125 mL
Mayonnaise	1 cup	250 mL
Powdered sugar	2 tbsp.	30 mL
Strawberries, mashed	¾ cup	175 mL

Whip cream until stiff. Fold in mayonnaise, sugar and strawberries. Makes scant 3 cups (750 mL).

SPINACH DRESSING

This is an excellent variation for spinach salad.

Garlic clove, minced	1	1
Salad oil	6 tbsp.	100 mL
Cider or red vinegar	2 tbsp.	30 mL
Granulated sugar	1 tsp.	5 mL
Dry mustard	1 tsp.	5 mL
Salt	1 tsp.	5 mL
Pepper	½ tsp.	2 mL

Mix together well. Pour over spinach salad.

Cobb Salad page 130

142

POPPY SEED DRESSING

Thick and fairly dark. Try it for a change.

Granulated sugar	¾ cup	175 mL
Dry mustard	1 tsp.	5 mL
Salt	1 tsp.	5 mL
Vinegar	⅓ cup	75 mL
Onion flakes	1 tsp.	5 mL
Salad oil	1 cup	225 mL
Poppy seeds	1½ tbsp.	25 mL
Red food coloring (optional)		

Put sugar, mustard, salt, vinegar and onion in blender. Blend until smooth.

Add salad oil in a slow steady stream beating all the time. Beat until thick.

Stir in poppy seeds and add enough coloring to make a pleasing pink color. Makes a large cupful.

CONDENSED MILK DRESSING

A good choice if you want the taste of vinegar without the strong flavor. Makes a great fruit dip.

Eggs, well beaten	2	2
Sweetened condensed milk	11 oz.	300 mL
Vinegar	½ cup	125 mL
Dry mustard	1 tsp.	5 mL

Beat eggs in medium bowl until frothy. Add condensed milk, vinegar and mustard. Blend together well. Serve with fruit. Makes 2⅓ cups (550 mL).

CIDER DRESSING: Omit vinegar. Add ¼ cup (50 mL) cider vinegar. Gives a sweeter, different flavor.

Pictured on page 71.

CREAM CHEESE FROSTING

Any salad would be happy to be dressed up with this. Makes a great dip for fruit.

Cream cheese	4 oz.	125 g
Mayonnaise	2 tbsp.	30 mL
Icing sugar	¼ cup	50 mL

Have cream cheese at room temperature. Beat all three ingredients together well. Serve with jellied salad, or use as accompaniment for fresh fruit salads.

PEANUT BUTTER DRESSING

A mellow peanut butter flavor.

Mayonnaise	¼ cup	50 mL
Liquid honey	1 tbsp.	15 mL
Peanut butter	1 tbsp.	15 mL

Mix all together. Serve over greens and fruit served together or separately. Makes about ⅓ cup (75 mL).

PEANUT BUTTER TOPPING: Omit mayonnaise. Increase quantity of honey and peanut butter, keeping amounts equal. Good peanut butter flavor. Serve over bananas, oranges, celery, etc.

CRANBERRY TOPPING

A most colorful topping for fruit salads.

Whole cranberry sauce	¾ cup	175 mL
Mayonnaise	¼ cup	50 mL
Lemon juice	1 tbsp.	15 mL
Granulated sugar	1 tbsp.	15 mL
Dry mustard	¼ tsp.	1 mL

Mix all five ingredients together well. Makes 1 cup (225 mL). Serve over cottage cheese and fruit.

FRENCH DRESSING

A regular well known type of dressing. Oily.

Vinegar	⅓ cup	75 mL
Salad oil	1 cup	225 mL
Granulated sugar	1 tsp.	5 mL
Paprika	1 tsp.	5 mL
Salt	1 tsp.	5 mL
Pepper	¼ tsp.	1 mL
Pinch of cayenne		

Put all seven ingredients in bottle. Cover and shake together well. Shake before using.

DOCTORED DRESSING

A very easy make-your-own recipe to have on hand.

Salad dressing	2 cups	500 mL
Sour cream	2 cups	500 mL
Granulated sugar	¼ cup	50 mL
Garlic powder	⅛ tsp.	½ mL
Paprika	½ tsp.	2 mL
Salt	½ tsp.	2 mL
Pepper (white is best)	⅛ tsp.	½ mL

Measure all seven ingredients in bowl. Stir to blend well. Store in covered container in refrigerator. Makes 4 cups (1L). May be used with green salads. Try a dollup on a jellied salad.

Paré Pointer

Success is doing something usual and doing it unusually well.

GROUP GOLDEN GLOW

About the most economical salad to serve a crowd as well as the most likely to be to everyone's liking. May be made a day or two ahead.

Water	8 cups	1.8 L
Lemon-flavored gelatin	16 – 3 oz.	16 – 85 g
Salt	2 tsp.	10 mL
Cold water	10 cups	2.25 L
Crushed pineapple and juice	10 – 14 oz.	10 – 398 mL
Chopped celery stock	1	1
Grated carrot	2 lbs.	1 kg

In large saucepan put water. Bring to boil over medium heat. Stir in gelatin and salt until dissolved. Remove from heat. Pour into large container. A plastic pail works well.

Add cold water, pineapple and juice. Chill until syrupy stirring now and then.

Fold in celery and carrot. Pour into smaller containers or molds or leave in pail for dishing up later. Chill overnight. Serves 125-150 along with another jellied salad.

GROUP COLESLAW

Prepare vegetables and dressing separately. Combine when ready to serve.

Cabbage, shredded	15 lbs.	7 kg
Carrots, grated	1 lb.	500 g
Coleslaw dressing (commercial)	6 cups	1.4 L
Celery seed	3 tbsp.	50 mL
Dry onion flakes	3 tbsp.	50 mL
Water	¼ cup	50 mL
Salt	2 tbsp.	30 mL

For easier mixing divide cabbage and carrots between two tubs. Chill.

Mix coleslaw dressing, celery seed, onion, water and salt together in bowl. Divide into two cartons. Chill until almost ready to serve. Pour over top of cabbage. Toss together well. It should coat well but if needed, more dressing may be added. Serves 100.

A large plastic tub for each one hundred people is a must for mixing. A snap to serve if tossed with Oil and Vinegar dressing, page 138, rather than using individual dressings.

Lettuce, large solid heads		
cut up	7	7
Bunches of green onions, sliced	2	2
Small red cabbage, shredded	1	1

Cut up lettuce into large plastic tub. Add sliced green onions. Add shredded red cabbage. Just before serving, pour equal amounts of oil and the vinegar-sugar mixture over top. Toss to coat, adding more oil and vinegar-sugar as needed.

Note: The above is an economical salad as well as being quick to prepare. If finances and time permit, additions may be added — sliced radishes, sliced or chopped green peppers, sliced celery, chopped cucumber.

GIANT TOMATO ASPIC

Very fast to prepare. Omit celery and apple or add only one of them. Amount can easily be increased or decreased. Make a day or two ahead.

Lemon-flavored gelatin	16 – 3 oz.	16 – 85 g
Hot water	8 cups	1.8 L
Salt	8 tsp.	40 mL
Pepper	½ tsp.	2 mL
Onion powder	4 tsp.	20 mL
Tomato juice	18 cups	4 L
Celery, chopped fine	4-5 cups	1 L
Apple, peeled and diced fine	4-5 cups	1 L

Combine gelatin and hot water in saucepan. Heat and stir over medium heat until dissolved. Remove from heat. Stir in salt, pepper and onion powder and pour into plastic pail or other large container.

Stir in tomato juice. Chill until syrupy, stirring occasionally.

Fold in celery and apple. Transfer to smaller containers or leave in pail for easy transporting to be dished up elsewhere. Chill several hours. As a second salad, serves 100-125.

PICNIC POTATO SALAD

This is a very quick recipe for a crowd which can be doubled or tripled with ease. One recipe is about all you can handle at once in a very large laundry type plastic tub.

Potatoes, cooked, cubed or coarsely mashed	33 lbs.	15 kg
Eggs, hard boiled and chopped	3 dozen	3 dozen
Salt	5⅓ tbsp.	75 mL
Pepper	2 tsp.	10 mL
Parsley flakes	½ cup	125 mL
Green onion flakes	¼ cup	50 mL
Dry white onion flakes	1½ cups	325 mL
Water	1½ cups	325 mL
Milk	2½ cups	575 mL
Salad Dressing	7 cups	1.6 L
Paprika		

Have potatoes and eggs prepared and chilled in advance. About 2-3 hours before serving combine with balance of ingredients.

In medium size bowl combine salt, pepper, parsley, green onion flakes and white onion flakes. Stir together well. Stir in water, milk and salad dressing. Refrigerate until ready to assemble. Then put chilled potatoes and eggs into large plastic tub. Pour salad dressing mixture over top. Combine together being sure to moisten all potatoes in the bottom of tub. Transfer to smaller tubs or large serving bowls. Sprinkle with paprika. Chill until serving time. Serves 100.

Note: Three dozen eggs is the minimum used. Up to ten dozen eggs may be used. Dry onion may be replaced with fresh minced onion. You will need triple the amount and if using, omit 1½ cups (325 mL) water.

It is all right to hold opinions but you are obstinate if opinions hold you.

METRIC CONVERSION

Throughout this book measurements are given in conventional and metric measure. To compensate for differences between the two measurements due to rounding, a full metric measure is not always used.

The cup used is the standard 8 fluid ounce.

Temperature is given in degrees Fahrenheit and Celsius.

Baking pan measurements are in inches and centimetres, as well as quarts and litres. An exact conversion is given below as well as the working equivalent.

Spoons	Exact Conversion	Standard Metric Measure
¼ teaspoon	1.2 millilitres	1 millilitre
½ teaspoon	2.4 millilitres	2 millilitres
1 teaspoon	4.7 millilitres	5 millilitres
2 teaspoons	9.4 millilitres	10 millilitres
1 tablespoon	14.2 millilitres	15 millilitres

Cups		
¼ cup (4 T)	56.8 millilitres	50 millilitres
⅓ cup (5⅓ T)	75.6 millilitres	75 millilitres
½ cup (8 T)	113.7 millilitres	125 millilitres
⅔ cup (10⅔ T)	151.2 millilitres	150 millilitres
¾ cup (12 T)	170.5 millilitres	175 millilitres
1 cup (16 T)	227.3 millilitres	250 millilitres
4½ cups	984.8 millilitres	1000 millilitres, 1 litre

Ounces — Weight		
1 oz.	28.3 grams	30 grams
2 oz.	56.7 grams	55 grams
3 oz.	85 grams	85 grams
4 oz.	113.4 grams	125 grams
5 oz.	141.7 grams	140 grams
6 oz.	170.1 grams	170 grams
7 oz.	198.4 grams	200 grams
8 oz.	226.8 grams	250 grams
16 oz.	453.6 grams	500 grams
32 oz.	917.2 grams	1000 grams, 1 kg

Pans, Casseroles

8 × 8 inch, 20 × 20 cm, 2L

9 × 9 inch, 22 × 22 cm, 2.5L

9 × 13 inch, 22 × 33 cm, 4L

10 × 15 inch, 25 × 38 cm, 1.2L

11 × 17 inch, 28 × 43 cm, 1.5L

8 × 2 inch round, 20 × 5 cm, 2L

9 × 2 inch round, 22 × 5 cm, 2.5L

10 × 4½ inch tube, 25 × 11 cm, 5L

8 × 4 × 3 inch loaf, 20 × 10 × 7 cm, 1.5L

9 × 5 × 3 inch loaf, 23 × 12 × 7 cm, 2L

Oven Temperatures

Fahrenheit	Celsius	Fahrenheit	Celsius	Fahrenheit	Celsius
175°	80°	300°	150°	425°	220°
200°	100°	325°	160°	450°	230°
225°	110°	350°	180°	475°	240°
250°	120°	375°	190°	500°	260°
275°	140°	400°	200°		

INDEX

(continued on next page)

(continued on next page)

153

(continued on next page)

**COMPANY'S COMING
PUBLISHING LIMITED
BOX 8037, STATION "F"
EDMONTON, ALBERTA,
CANADA T6H 4N9**

COOKBOOKS

Please send the following cookbooks to the address on the reverse side of this coupon.

ENGLISH		
TITLE (Hard Cover @ $17.95 each)	**QUANTITY**	**AMOUNT**
JEAN PARÉ'S FAVORITES		
VOLUME ONE - 232 pages		
TITLE (Soft Cover @ $10.95 each)		
150 DELICIOUS SQUARES		
CASSEROLES		
MUFFINS & MORE		
SALADS		
APPETIZERS		
DESSERTS		
SOUPS & SANDWICHES		
HOLIDAY ENTERTAINING		
COOKIES		
VEGETABLES		
MAIN COURSES		
PASTA		
CAKES		
BARBECUES		
DINNERS OF THE WORLD		
(September, 1991)		

FRENCH		
TITLE (Soft Cover @ $10.95 each)		
150 DÉLICIEUX CARRÉS		
LES CASSEROLES		
MUFFINS ET PLUS		
TOTAL ALL BOOKS		$

- **SAVE $5.00**
  Order any 2 cookbooks by mail at regular prices and SAVE $5.00 on every third cookbook per order.

- *Prices subject to change without prior notice.*

- *Sorry, no C.O.D.'s*

- **ORDERS OUTSIDE CANADA:**
  Must be paid in U.S. funds by cheque or money order drawn on Canadian or U.S. bank.

- **MAKE CHEQUE OR MONEY ORDER PAYABLE TO:**
  COMPANY'S COMING PUBLISHING LIMITED

TOTAL COST OF BOOKS	$
LESS $5.00 for every third book per order	−
PLUS $1.50 postage & handling per book	+
SUB TOTAL	$
Canadian residents add GST	+
TOTAL AMOUNT ENCLOSED	$

↓   GIFT CARD MESSAGE   ↓

- - - - - - - - - - - - - - -

A GIFT FOR YOU

Company's Coming **COOKBOOKS**

Company's Coming COOKBOOKS

A NATIONAL BEST SELLER

I would like to order the Company's Coming Cookbooks listed on the reverse side of this coupon.

NAME_____
(PLEASE PRINT)

STREET_____

CITY _____

PROVINCE/STATE _____ POSTAL CODE/ZIP _____

GIFT GIVING – WE MAKE IT EASY...
... YOU MAKE IT DELICIOUS!

Let us help you with your gift giving! We will send cookbooks directly to the recipients of your choice if you give us their names and addresses. Be sure to specify the titles of the cookbooks you wish to send to each person.

Enclose a personal note or card for each gift or use our handy gift card below.

Company's Coming Cookbooks are the perfect gift for birthdays, showers, Mother's Day, Father's Day, graduation or any occasion ... collect them all!

Don't forget to take advantage of the **$5.00 saving ... buy any two Company's Coming Cookbooks by mail and save $5.00 on every third copy per order.**

↓   GIFT CARD MESSAGE   ↓

COMPANY'S COMING
PUBLISHING LIMITED
BOX 8037, STATION "F"
EDMONTON, ALBERTA,
CANADA T6H 4N9

COOKBOOKS

Please send the following cookbooks to the address on the reverse side of this coupon.

ENGLISH		
TITLE (Hard Cover @ $17.95 each)	**QUANTITY**	**AMOUNT**
JEAN PARÉ'S FAVORITES		
VOLUME ONE - 232 pages		
TITLE (Soft Cover @ $10.95 each)		
150 DELICIOUS SQUARES		
CASSEROLES		
MUFFINS & MORE		
SALADS		
APPETIZERS		
DESSERTS		
SOUPS & SANDWICHES		
HOLIDAY ENTERTAINING		
COOKIES		
VEGETABLES		
MAIN COURSES		
PASTA		
CAKES		
BARBECUES		
DINNERS OF THE WORLD		
(September, 1991)		

FRENCH		
TITLE (Soft Cover @ $10.95 each)		
150 DÉLICIEUX CARRÉS		
LES CASSEROLES		
MUFFINS ET PLUS		
TOTAL ALL BOOKS		$

■ **SAVE $5.00**

Order any 2 cookbooks by mail at regular prices and SAVE $5.00 on every third cookbook per order.

■ *Prices subject to change without prior notice.*

■ *Sorry, no C.O.D.'s*

■ **ORDERS OUTSIDE CANADA:**
Must be paid in U.S. funds by cheque or money order drawn on Canadian or U.S. bank.

■ **MAKE CHEQUE OR MONEY ORDER PAYABLE TO:**
COMPANY'S COMING PUBLISHING LIMITED

TOTAL COST OF BOOKS	$
LESS $5.00 for every third book per order	–
PLUS $1.50 postage & handling per book	+
SUB TOTAL	$
Canadian residents add GST	+
TOTAL AMOUNT ENCLOSED	$

↓   **GIFT CARD MESSAGE**   ↓

Company's Coming
COOKBOOKS

A GIFT FOR YOU

Company's Coming
COOKBOOKS

I would like to order the Company's Coming Cookbooks listed on the reverse side of this coupon.

NAME_____
(PLEASE PRINT

STREET_____

CITY _____

PROVINCE/STATE _____ POSTAL CODE/ZIP _____

GIFT GIVING – WE MAKE IT EASY...
... YOU MAKE IT DELICIOUS!

Let us help you with your gift giving! We will send cookbooks directly to the recipients of your choice if you give us their names and addresses. Be sure to specify the titles of the cookbooks you wish to send to each person.

Enclose a personal note or card for each gift or use our handy gift card below.

Company's Coming Cookbooks are the perfect gift for birthdays, showers, Mother's Day, Father's Day, graduation or any occasion ... collect them all!

Don't forget to take advantage of the **$5.00 saving ... buy any two Company's Coming Cookbooks by mail and save $5.00 on every third copy per order.**

↓　　　GIFT CARD MESSAGE　　　↓